Country Roads

~ of ~

HAWAII

A Guide Book
from Country Roads Press

Country Roads
~ of ~
HAWAII

Robert Wenkam

Illustrated by
Ned Schwartz

Country Roads Press
CASTINE • MAINE

Country Roads of Hawaii

Published by Country Roads Press
P.O. Box 286, Lower Main Street
Castine, Maine 04421

Text and cover design by Edith Allard.
Illustrations by Ned Schwartz.

Library of Congress Cataloging-in-Publication Data
Wenkam, Robert, 1920–
    Country Roads of Hawaii / Robert Wenkam :
illustrated by Ned Schwartz.
        p.   cm.
    Includes bibliographical references and index.
    ISBN 1-56626-031-0 : $9.95
        1. Hawaii—Description and travel—1981–   2. Rural
roads—Hawaii—Description and travel.   I. Title.
DU623.25.W46   1993
919.6904'4—dc20   92-22775
                                                CIP

Printed in the United States of America.
10 9 8 7 6 5 4 3 2 1

For my children,
Chiye, Miyo, Jay, and Tad

Contents

(& Key to Hawaii Country Roads)

Introduction

I first rode around the Big Island of Hawaii when it was very difficult to do so—in the spring of 1943, with a war on. The trip from Hilo to Volcano to Kona to Waimea and back to Hilo took an entire week. It took one day just to find a taxi driver in Kona willing to sacrifice a week's ration of gasoline to drive me from Kailua to Waimea. After a little hitchhiking, I caught the daily train at Paauilo, in Hamakua, to complete my trip to Hilo by rail. I met no other travelers. (The train no longer exists.)

In those days there were no rental cars, and places to eat, apart from the handful of hotels that were taking guests, were few and far between. Coming out to greet me when I arrived at his hotel an hour late for dinner, the Kona Inn manager remarked, "I knew how you were coming—by banana wagon. Your dinner is waiting." I ate alone.

The following year I made my first trip on Maui's Hana Road, behind the stake truck delivering mail and bread on its weekly run from Kahului. I first rode to Lahaina clinging to the floor of a flatbed truck traveling the old one-lane road. On my first visit to Kauai, I walked across the island to Hanalei, after camping in Puhi, near Lihue. On our first date, in 1941, a local girl on Oahu revealed to me that she had never been to the other side of the island—so that's where we went on our next date. We drove clear around the island.

Rental cars and restaurants did not become abundant until the mid-1950s. With Hawaii's statehood, investment capital poured into the local economy, and tourist service businesses boomed. Driving soon became a habit-forming pleasure on the steadily expanding state highway system, and fast-food outlets sprang up on every corner to cater to hungry tourists. Today, on almost any popular road, half the cars may be rental units. Hawaii is ready for the armchair traveler and the rental car, with nearly every island road now paved.

A few comments are in order about renting cars in Hawaii, since this will be your only way of getting around. For the best rates, reserve your choice of car well in advance and by the week. The same company will take care of you on every island. Remember that most personal auto insurance policies and personal credit cards do not cover travel by four-wheel drive. The fine print in many Hawaii rental contracts allows the agency to cancel the agreement if a car is driven on unpaved roads—so be careful driving on dirt. It's very expensive to return your car to a place other than the one you rented from—or without a full tank of gas.

Most Big Island car rental people say no to driving across the island on the Saddle Road, because you're just too far away from help if you stall in that part of the world. (I heard of one visitor who paid $200 for a tow truck.) If you plan on driving to the summit of Mauna Kea, ask the rental agent if your car can make it to the 13,796-foot summit. Be alert and careful at tourist parking lots at Akaka Falls, Ke'e, and other remote locations, leaving in your car only what you can live without. Drive down the long, steep grades from Mauna Kea and Haleakala in second gear to save your brakes.

I don't mention all my favorite places to stay and eat, unless the food or accommodations strike me as being particularly good or the area has few of either to offer. Nor have I said much about prices, because they change so quickly.

Good road maps are free at every rental car agency, but it is practically impossible to get lost driving the islands. All the roads go up or down and around—part way. Most of the time it is simply a case of turning around and returning to your starting point. No island has a passable road going all the way around it. When you arrive at cinder or dirt, the best policy is to turn around and go back.

Fill the gas tank before returning your car. Gas sells by the liter in the islands and costs about the same everywhere, so you gain nothing by trying to calculate the price per gallon. You won't need oil. It will probably rain at night, so washing the car will be unnecessary. The rest is up to you.

I have driven all the roads of Hawaii in the last few months, and I can confirm that there is no other island in the world that is such a pleasure to drive. Or so beautiful. Enjoy your journey of discovery in the islands of Hawaii!

Note: A glossary of Hawaiian words is provided on page 115. To simplify road designations, I've used the following abbreviations: I = Interstate; US = US Route or Highway; State = State Route or Highway.

1 ~

Kauai's

North

Shore

Princeville-
Hanalei-
Haena-Ke'e

How to get there: About an hour's drive north out of the town of Lihue, through Kapaa, and past the Kilauea intersection on State 56 is the entrance to Princeville. Here we begin driving the fabulous north shore.

Highlights: *Hanalei Valley overlook; old Hawaii atmosphere in Hanalei; the Waioli Mission House; Waikoko Beach; "Bali Hai" Beach; the Limahuli branch of the National Tropical Botanical Garden; Dry and Wet Caves; the Na Pali Coast; a sacred shrine to the goddess of the hula; full moon at Ke'e Beach.*

A drive through Princeville forms an excellent introduction to the old Hawaii, providing as it does a definite transition from luxury resorts to the simple, old-style rural life enjoyed in the valley below. Bulldozers began working here in 1969, when the Colorado oil company that developed Vail purchased Princeville cattle ranchlands from Amfac to do the same job in Hawaii.

The oil company hired me to photograph the scenic area. During my first meeting with the developers, I could only think of ways to stop the project from continuing. Standing in the middle of the untouched ranch, I argued that the land

1

should be part of the great Kauai national park I was promoting at the time. They told me that for a price—$17 million—they would stop development and sell the land back for a park. Nowhere was that kind of money available for parklands, so the biggest development on Kauai proceeded as planned. Picture, if you can, the three championship golf courses, the tennis courts, major hotels, and fancy condominiums as the grand entrance to a great national park.

A beautiful beach that I have often photographed is Kenomene at the foot of the north *pali* (cliff), reached by a short walk from the parking lot of Pali Ke Kua condominiums. A picnic pavilion is located on the terrace, but I have always carried lunch with me to the beach below, bearing in mind that during the winter months high surf sometimes sweeps completely over the sands.

Outside the entrance to Princeville, where State 56 becomes State 560, you come upon what is perhaps the most famous view on Kauai: the Hanalei Valley overlook, with its magnificent panorama of geometric-patterned taro patches and the winding Hanalei River. The Hawaiians first saw this valley a thousand years ago. The spectacle of its rainbows and mists, generated by an annual rainfall in excess of 100 inches a year, continues to enchant to this day. Hawaiians first grew taro here for poi (a Hawaiian dish of taro root cooked, pounded, and kneaded to a paste), then the Chinese grew rice until cheaper California rice became available. Later, Japanese farmers began growing taro for the Hawaiians.

I realized that the developers' purchase of Amfac ranchlands included Hanalei Valley, and urged that the one-year leases then in effect be extended to ten years or more so that the farmers could borrow funds to put their taro-growing operation on a more businesslike basis. This was done, and the growers immediately purchased tractors and expanded their acreage of taro, keeping the valley in the traditional first Hawaiian crop.

When it was found that the Hawaiian duck and stilt and the endangered Hawaiian gallinule were compatible with taro growing, these lands were quickly designated the Hanalei National Wildlife Refuge. For a close-up look at this ancient place of birds and taro, drive up Ohiki Road at the bridge turnoff and travel back in time.

Looking straight down from the edge of the overlook, you will see the old, one-way, steel girder bridge, a cultural dam that over the years has prevented Hanalei and the lands beyond from being engulfed by tourism and condominiums. For over forty years residents of the valley have successfully resisted the attempts of the state highway department to replace the bridge and widen the highway. They have insisted their part of the world remain just the way it is—somewhat old-fashioned, undeveloped, and inconvenient. As a result, the single-lane highway and old bridges—many of them partially collapsed following early tsunami waves—are still in use, all the way to the curving end of the road at Ke'e Beach.

Local etiquette requires that all cars approaching one of these old bridges wait until the bridge clears completely from the other side before crossing. Also, you will never hear any horns honking. It's part of the rural charm of Hanalei.

It is impossible to comment about places of interest in the town of Hanalei at this writing, only months after Hurricane Iniki swept the island of Kauai, destroying or seriously damaging almost every business and home along the highway. We can only hope that most will have been rebuilt by the time you visit the area. Even in these difficult circumstances, the residents of this ramshackle community will be friendly. In Hanalei even the new somehow seems old. The green *pali* behind forms a sort of frontier between Hanalei and the rest of the world. The north shore road we travel spans the cultural gap between civilization and wilderness.

3

At the end of the road, where sand pushes hard against craggy cliffs, Hawaiians launched outrigger canoes into the surf to reach isolated hanging valleys beyond Kalalau. Hanalei became a refuge from the contemporary world, a place discovered by Polynesians, civilized by the missionaries, and settled by those who prefer living at the end of the road.

Between Tahiti Nui and the Black Pot Restaurant, the side road, Aku, leads to Hanalei Bay past the Beach Park Pavilion, where windsurfers launch their craft, ending at Hanalei River, where Na Pali Coast Tours launch their boats. (The road changes its name to Weke Road near the end.) On the left is Hanalei Pier, built in 1890 for loading rice on interisland ships. Adjacent is Black Pot Beach, which in recent years has been the late-night hangout where local fishermen prepare their fish, eat, drink, and "talk story."

Back on the highway, behind the green, shingled Waioli Huiia Church, is Waioli Mission House, on the National Register of Historic Places. The home of the first missionary in Hanalei, Reverend William Alexander, this building is well worth a visit.

Gas up, if necessary, in Hanalei. There are no gas stations beyond this point. At the western end of town is the first of several old, one-way bridges you will encounter. Watch for opposing traffic. There isn't very much.

Where the road climbs ahead and turns left is Waikoko Beach, easily the most beautiful beach on Kauai and the most photographed. Park in a wide part of the road and walk up the hill to capture the scene through lacy pandanus trees. Waikoko is the beach where Mitzi Gaynor washed that man out of her hair in the movie *South Pacific*. During the summer months, when the surf is not dangerous, walk down the slippery trail for lunch and a romantic afternoon. Swimming off Waikoko Beach is not advisable at any time of the year, because there is no reef to cancel out riptides and undertow.

Where Mitzi Gaynor washed that man right out of her hair

In the next valley, across a "temporary" one-way bridge, is the town of Wainiha, which has an old general store where you can stop, if only for a cold Coke and a chat with the owners or local people hanging around. Beyond the store are two more "temporary" wood bridges built to replace those destroyed by the thirty-foot tsunami wave that swept through here in 1957. After the bridges you'll come to a side road up Wainiha Valley to McBryde's powerhouse and a fabulous private trail crossing the island.

Shortly before you reach the Dry Cave, where a stream crosses over the highway, a narrow dirt road leads to a parking area in the ironwoods that backs onto a beach locally called Makua. This is the northern reach of Haena Beach, "Bali Hai" Beach in the movie *South Pacific*, where Bloody Mary did her bit. Haena Bay is swimmable only on calm summer days, but it is a great place for a picnic or sunbathing. Walk into the Dry Cave to cool off.

Farther along, around a couple of curves and on your left is Limahuli Valley, where the road fords Limahuli Stream. The large garden you see a short distance into the valley is part of the National Tropical Botanical Garden. Tours are free for members. Nonmembers pay an admission fee. Reservations are necessary for both members and nonmembers. Because of hurricane damage, the Limahuli garden will not reopen until the fall of 1993, at the very earliest.

The swimming hole next to the highway is a favorite stop for hikers coming off the Kalalau Trail. Unlike the ocean, the water here is very cold and refreshing.

Across the way is the site of the infamous Taylor Camp, where Elizabeth Taylor's brother allowed a tree village of hippies and friends to grow in the 1960s. The area was later condemned and added to the lands of Haena State Park.

Past Waikapalae Wet Cave, next to Waikanaloa Wet Cave, at highway level, you'll find the beach and lagoon at Ke'e and the beginning of the spectacular Kalalau and Hanakapiai trails. A half-mile walk on this trail will reveal unrivaled splendors and a long view of the Na Pali Coast and Ke'e Beach. It's a long way to Kalalau Valley from here, about fifteen miles, a full day as most measure the trail, but I once walked in and out in one day to see if it could be done. With no packs it is possible.

On the way to Kalalau, about three miles in, is Hanakapiai Bay, where more tourists have drowned than anywhere else on Kauai. Don't even think of swimming here.

The old Allerton home, once nestled against the slope above Ke'e Beach, has burned, but the path in front leads to an even older historical site, claimed by some to be one of the most sacred spots in all Hawaii: Kaulu-Paoa Heiau, the *heiau* (shrine) where Pele, the fire goddess, taught Hawaiians the hula. On this site is a shrine to Laka, goddess of the hula. Approach the *heiau* with reverence.

Protected by a reef, Ke'e Beach, at the end of the road, is swimmable almost any day of the year, and the crowds of tourists you'll encounter at midday confirm this. I recommend a visit in the evening, at full moon, when the beach will undoubtedly be all yours. Stroll to the right in the sand, out to where the full length of the Na Pali Coast gradually appears in view, and revel in one of the most glorious places on earth.

In the Area

All numbers are within area code 808.

National Tropical Botanical Garden, Limahuli branch: 826-5547

2 ~

Kauai's High Country:

Waimea Canyon-Kokee-Kalalau Lookout

How to get there: On the southern shore, on the western edge of the town of Waimea, disregard the highway sign that says "Straight ahead to Waimea Canyon," and take a sharp right onto the residential street that almost immediately starts to wind up the hillside into mountain country. On your right is the great, multihued Waimea Canyon, which becomes deeper and more spectacular as you ascend.

Highlights: *Waimea Canyon, described by Mark Twain as "the Grand Canyon of the Pacific"; Kukui Trail and the Iliau Nature Loop; Waialae Falls; Alakai Swamp; botanical wonders; the Kokee Natural History Museum; Kokee Cabins; Kalalau Valley Lookout.*

Across the way, delineating grand views of the canyon, you see the edge of Alakai Swamp. Beyond sugarcane fields, in the opposite direction, you take in a grand panorama of the western shore of Kauai and distant Niihau Island. The narrow road, which widens enough in places to accommodate the few passing cars, winds upward into a jumbled tropical forest of exotic trees planted many years ago by plantation agriculturists to create an island watershed. The irrigation ditches you pass over are full of water carried from higher Alakai Swamp, evidence of their success in providing water for lowland sugarcane growers.

8

Shortly after passing the old road junction, on the right side of a widening in the road with space for parking, is the beginning of Kukui Trail into Waimea Canyon and the Iliau Nature Loop. A stroll on the loop is an education in tropical plant life, even though many plant labels are missing. (The iliau is related to the silversword of Maui.)

The main Kukui Trail, the only trail into the canyon, is graded all the way to the bottom, but the lower portion is overgrown, and the two-hour descent grows to over three sweaty hours on the climb back up to your car. Allow for even more time on a hot summer day, for it is dry and arid in the canyon and the 2,000-foot difference in elevation makes for a complete change in weather and temperature. Views of Waimea Canyon and Waialae Falls from trail lookouts will more than reward your efforts, but follow the cairns and trail markers carefully if you plan on finding the way back to your parking place on Kokee Highway.

I've camped in the canyon along the Waimea River several times and enjoyed swimming in the river, but only once have I hiked the Kukui Trail upward. I chose to take the long way out and followed the river trail. Once we came across a ditch tender's cabin we had never seen before, found a working telephone on the *lanai* (porch), and called for a Papillon helicopter to pick us up. Expensive, but nice.

Trails follow the canyon floor for miles along the river. The Koaie Canyon across the way can be hiked all the way to the edge of Alakai Swamp to a great camping site near a swimming hole.

The turnoff to Waimea Canyon Lookout is well marked. Here is the grand view of the canyon, the most photographed and awe-inspiring panorama. Plan to stay a while. Lean on the railing and let your gaze drift. The canyon is one mile wide, ten miles long, and 3,000 feet deep. Across at the same elevation is the edge of Alakai Swamp, divided by three tributary canyons—Poomau, Koaie, and Waialae—all hikable and with streams flowing all year long. Almost any words you can think of for this great vista will be inadequate.

Farther along the road, you'll find other scenic lookouts into the canyon, none any better than what you will have already seen. Roads to the left go to private homes, summer camps, trails, and a Navy Missile Range facility. Gates to NASA Tracking Station facilities open on both sides of the road as you near the Kokee cabins, the Lodge restaurant, and Kokee Natural History Museum. The museum offers (at no charge) an excellent introduction to local plants and wildlife in the park area and provides the latest trail and road maps to Na Pali ridges and into Alakai Swamp. Cabins should be reserved long in advance. Kokee has everything but a market, so bring all you need with you or plan to eat at the Lodge.

Unpaved roads on the right (passable only in dry weather) lead to many trails along the rim of Waimea Canyon and farther on into Alakai Swamp country, where more trails bring the hiker into the wet country. It is possible to camp in the swamp and hike all the way to the summit of Mount Waialeale, but without a guide who knows the area it is not considered safe to do so. I've been lost in the swamp myself and can testify that without carrying several days' worth of food and camping gear, and without the stamina to slog through deep mud and absorb all-day heavy rain, you will not find the expedition a pleasant one. The Sierra Club Hawaii Service Trip Program is now building an Alakai Swamp boardwalk into this area to make it easier for the less experienced hiker to discover "the wettest spot on earth."

Here and there in the wilderness of Kauai—and this wilderness is all about you in Kokee—local individuals cultivate a plant known to Hawaiians as *pakalolo* (marijuana). Entering these planted areas, even accidentally, is potentially dangerous; the growers use deadly force to protect their crops. Familiarize yourself with the plant's appearance so that you can avoid trouble.

10

Methley plums, which ripen toward the end of May, attract many families to the park trails. Also abundant are blackberries and passion fruit vines; the best time to pick the fruit and the location of the best bearers are much-discussed topics among local residents. Some will wait for plums to ripen in hidden parts of the forest and arrive with everything necessary to strip a plum tree in a few hours.

The tropical jungle includes many plants that came to the islands as cultivated varieties and eventually escaped their containers or garden borders to spread through the forest. The bright nasturtiums you see were first planted in the yard of a mountain cabin at Halemanu. Construction workers planted the hanging pink lilikoi around their dormitories for food while digging the Kekaha irrigation tunnels in 1923. Calla lilies were first seen at about the same time. Monthretia, a small bright-red lily, was well established by 1905. The purple-flowered "Isenberg bush" was brought to Kauai from the foothills of the Himalayas by Dora Isenberg and carefully tended in her garden. The attractive tibouchina plant soon escaped from her Lihue home and spread first to the foothills of Kilohana and then to Kokee.

Mrs. Abner Wilcox brought from Honolulu a small, multiblossomed lantana potted in a red bowl. She enjoyed the tiny orange and pink blossoms for many years until the plant grew too large for her porch. Her gardener threw it out on the trash pile, from which it eventually spread to all parts of the island. The bush thrived on Kauai and grew into impenetrable thickets on dry ridges and flats laid bare by goats and cattle.

Guava, another exotic, also grew into thickets of trees, gradually choking out competing indigenous plant life. Java plum filled gulches from rim to rim, displacing native plants. The native forest was slowly and irretrievably replaced by a synthetic forest gathered from around the world. It is this new forest cover that constitutes the botanical Hawaii of today.

11

Continuing higher in the forest, you'll pass the beginnings of what are perhaps the two best trails up here, Awaawapuhi and Honopu trails, both leading down exciting ridge routes overlooking hanging valleys of Na Pali. These are perfect trails for less experienced hikers seeking beauty and quiet.

As you approach Kalalau Valley Lookout, you come to the 150th Aircraft Control and Warning Radar of the Hawaii Air National Guard, an incongruous installation in the park. The park staff originally wanted to plant redwood trees around the site, but were eventually persuaded to abandon the idea. Wild ginger and other tropical plants are now abundant in the area.

The most spectacular view of Kalalau Valley is at the lookout site. No need to drive farther. If you have the desire to venture closer, one of the most exciting trails along the valley rim begins at the edge, just to the left of the lookout, below the sign that says "No hiking/Dangerous cliffs/Keep out." Keep in mind that the farther you go, the more dangerous the trail becomes. What may be the world's best place to sit and dream awaits you. Be sure to bring a companion along to share paradise—you will not want to return soon.

Jack London described Kalalau best when he wrote of Koolau the leper:

> And over these things Koolau was king. And this was his kingdom,—a flower-throttled gorge, with beetling cliffs and crags, from which floated the blattings of wild goats. On three sides the grim walls rose, festooned in fantastic draperies of tropic vegetation and pierced by cave entrances—the rocky lairs of Koolau's subjects. On the fourth side the earth fell away into a tremendous abyss, and, far below, could be seen the summits of lesser peaks and crags, at whose bases foamed and rumbled the Pacific surge. In fine weather

Kalalau Valley in Nadoh State Park

a boat could land on the rocky beach that marked the entrance of Kalalau Valley, but the weather must be very fine. And a cool-headed mountaineer might climb from the beach to the head of Kalalau Valley, to this pocket among the peaks where Koolau ruled; but such a mountaineer must be very cool of head, and he must know the wild-goat trails well.

I brought Stewart Udall, President Carter's secretary of the interior, to the edge of this beauty on a very cloudy day, knowing well from past visits that after a short wait in the fog the clouds would drift away. They did, as if by magic, and we both watched in awe as the cloud-filled valley emptied before our eyes and a rainbow arched across the distant *pali*. Far below, ocean waves touched the shore. Mr. Udall was silent for a moment and then exclaimed, "Nowhere in the entire national park system is there scenic beauty like this! Give me the proclamation," he urged. "I'll sign it now."

But the timid Hawaiian congressional delegation did not introduce a bill. The manager of the Kauai Chamber of Commerce at the time opposed the national park and advanced an unusual argument, claiming that "the resulting publicity would attract too many tourists."

In the Area

All numbers are within area code 808.

Kokee Lodge and Cabins: 335-6061
Kokee Museum (and guides to Alakai Swamp): 335-9975
Kokee State Park: 335-5871

3 ~

Kauai's Sunny Shore:

Poipu-Lawai-Hanapepe-Salt Pond

How to get there: After exploring Poipu, take the only road out of town to Koloa. Take the main Koloa Road (530) to the junction of State 50, and continue west to Kalaheo. From Kalaheo to Hanapepe is only a few miles.

Highlights: *Poipu's luxury resorts and beaches; the Plantation Garden Restaurant; shave ice in Koloa; the National Tropical Botanical Garden at Lawai; the Olu Pua Botanical Gardens; heiaus and Shimonishi orchid nursery in Hanapepe; passionfruit frozen daiquiris at the Green Garden Cafe; traditional salt making.*

Make no mistake about it, Hurricane Iniki, which swept Kauai in 1992, devastated the island. Very little escaped. The island is still recovering; a year, even two, is too short a time to expect things to have returned to normal. Even the leaves on the trees, which grow back in great abundance almost immediately, do not yet have branches to grow on. The branches were blown away.

There has been no damage to the aloha spirit, however. In fact, it may be stronger than ever as the residents rebuild. Kauai's great natural beauty has been little touched and waits patiently for you. Flowers are again in bloom. Although many great trees lie on the ground, the new vistas they have revealed lend extra excitement to casual sightseeing.

Most businesses have resumed operation. To keep everyone informed, a telephone hotline offers up-to-date information on accommodations, activities, restaurants, car rentals, and other tourist services. Call toll-free, 1-800-262-1400, anytime.

Poipu on the sunny south shore is where most Kauai vacationers begin to explore the island, because Poipu is where most of the hotels are located, alongside swimmable beaches, calm seas, and riotous plant life. This is the region where commercial sugar growing began in Hawaii. Luxury resorts, restaurants, and tennis courts have turned the area into a tourist destination from which it is hard to wander.

Up on Kipuka Street, in a residential neighborhood, is a wonderful place to stay: Pua Hale, a deluxe house in a fenced, private garden. Call 1-800-745-7414 to reserve rooms. The owners are longtime residents who know everything about the island.

Poipu offers many excellent restaurants—some expensive, some moderate (budget-priced restaurants are as rare as unicorns). In the expensive category, the Plantation Garden Restaurant, on Poipu Road across from Kiahuna Plantation condos, occupies an old, open-air sugar planter's house, surrounded by a superb cactus garden planted by the owner in his retirement days. The staff serves dinner only, in the grand style. If you would like to dine in a tropical garden, this is where to go. Arrive early and stroll among the cactus.

Poipu extends all the way from where the road ends at Makahuena Point, at the site of Kauai's last volcanic eruption, to Spouting Horn in the opposite direction at the entrance to Lawai Valley. Here the sea pushes up like a geyser through a shoreline lava tube below a county parking lot, where spaces are hard to find. Assume that the seashell and souvenir vendors will have beaten you to the draw. The moaning sounds coming from beneath the lava are said to be the cries of a legendary lizard that crawled into the tube long ago and became trapped. Others say it is the moaning of Kauai county politicians wondering what to do about all the itinerant merchants crowding their viewpoint parking lot.

Inland, on the only road out of Poipu, is the town of Koloa, site of Hawaii's first sugar mill, now a refurbished and very commercial tourist shopping street. Koloa looks quite gaudy at night, with lights flashing from the eaves of every building. At the far end of town, on each side of the post office, are enough churches and temples to satisfy most spiritual needs. About halfway back down the picturesque main street you'll find a country store selling excellent shave ice. On a hot day, ask for a "rainbow." Where the road from Lihue enters Koloa there is a memorial park commemorating the early sugar growers and founders of the town.

Take the main Koloa Road (State 530) up to the junction of State 50, the round-the-island highway, then continue on to Kalaheo. At the top of the hill, at the signals, turn left on Papalina Road and drive to the end. At Kukuiolono Park (well worth a visit on your return), on the *mauka* (inland) side of the hill is the only golf course in Hawaii where you can play barefoot.

At the end of the road, turn into the parking area of the National Tropical Botanical Garden, a must for anyone touring Kauai. Tours of the gardens last about two to three hours and cost $15 a person for nonmembers; members do not pay admission. The gardens are open only to guided tours arranged through the visitors center of the botanical garden. As with the Limahuli garden, hurricane damage has closed the garden for repairs until the fall of 1993. Call the botanical garden at 808-332-7361 or write to P.O. Box 340, Lawai, Kauai, HI 96765.

A nonprofit educational and scientific center chartered by act of Congress, this is the premier tropical botanical research garden in the nation, mandated to collect and preserve endangered plant life from the tropical world. Included in the 186 acres is the Allerton estate spread, a fabulous garden within Lawai Valley.

Back on the main highway, heading west, you come to the sign for the Olu Pua Botanical Gardens at the top of the next hill after leaving the gulch beyond Kalaheo. These aren't as spectacular as the Allerton Gardens, and there's a hefty admission fee. The owners provide a map to guide visitors through the several gardens, which surround an old plantation manager's home. Olu Pua is a beautiful place to spend what's left of the afternoon.

At the road junction across from the Olu Pua entrance, take the Plantation Road (State 54) down to see the McBryde Sugar Mill on your way to Hanapepe. Turn off the main highway, bearing right to enter the main street under a large monkeypod tree at the entrance to town. Park and walk.

Hanapepe bears some resemblance to Koloa before it underwent gentrification. You'll find this vintage village—with its wooden sidewalks and weather-beaten storefronts—much as it was in the plantation days. Some abandoned stores were simply blown away by Iniki and will never be replaced. For a good idea of what life was like in the old days, find Awawa Road across the river and walk along the old farm lanes to appreciate the rickety cottages, local color, and carefully tended farms in Hanapepe Valley. You'll discover four *heiaus* (shrines) and many Hawaiian homesites. Try the pedestrian bridge across the river, and check out fighting cocks in nearby pens.

Find the feed store and Shimonishi orchid nursery, where 1,600 varieties of orchids are wholesaled to various markets. If you see something you like, the owner might sell it to you at retail. He'll explain how to care for your orchid so it makes the trip home in good shape.

Only in Hilo and Hanapepe did any violence occur during the historic 1924 sugar strike. Sixteen Filipino workers were killed by police in Hanapepe. The independent spirit of residents struggling for better working conditions still pervades this proud little town.

Step into the Hanapepe Bookstore & Espresso Bar for a vegetarian lunch or snack and browse through the new owners' fascinating collection of island-made gifts. Or try Hanapepe's inexpensive Green Garden cafe, which has been in the Hamabata family since it opened in 1948. Gwen Hamabata runs the place the same way her parents did. The cafe is a tropical jungle, with ferns hanging above and nestled below, and blooming orchids on every table. Gwen likes special requests, so if you're inclined, call her first (335-5422) and ask for something unusual for dinner. You will enjoy whatever she dreams up. By the way, the Green Garden is the only place in the world where you can find a passion-fruit frozen daiquiri. To get there, head back to the highway, but turn left instead of crossing the river.

After leaving the Green Garden, on the way to Salt Pond Beach, you will pass Lappert's Aloha Ice Cream and Kauai Cookies store, where Lappert's ice cream and cookies are made. Salt Pond Beach Park is a local beach, crowded with noisy families on weekends and holidays. Here is a great place to experience the island world. On the far end of the beach can be seen the Port Allen Airport runway, where after landing I found it easy to taxi my Cessna over to the sandy edge, just a short hop from the surf. Camping for the night was always a great pleasure at Salt Pond.

The road leading to the park pavilion passes numerous salt ponds dating back hundreds of years. Forty-seven families, the Hui Hana Paakai o Hanapepe, hold hereditary rights to these ancestral plots. Captain Cook described the salt-making process when he first landed in Hawaii and obtained his own salt at Salt Pond. The same methods are still in use today. Hawaiians mix the salt with red earth obtained from the summit of Waialeale and regard the result as very tasty. The county health people won't allow them to sell their salt in the market, so you may want to bargain for some of your own when visiting Salt Pond. The dirty salt tastes best.

In the Area

All numbers are within area code 808.

Plantation Garden Restaurant: 742-1695

National Tropical Botanical Garden: 332-7361

Golf course at Kukuiolono: 332-9151

Ola Pua Botanical Garden: 332-8182

Shimonishi Orchid Nursery: 335-5562

Hanapepe Bookstore and Espresso Bar: 335-5011

Green Garden Cafe: 335-5422

Lappert's Ice Cream, Hanapepe: 335-6121

Kauai Cookies Co.: 335-3291

4 ~

Oahu's Surfing Shore:

Kahuku-Waimea Beach-Haleiwa-Kaena

How to get there: Follow State 83 to Kahuku, Waimea, and Haleiwa. Outside Haleiwa, take State 930 west past Dillingham Air Force Base. When the paved road ends, park and hike the rest of the way to Kaena Point.

Highlights: *A cafe in a former sugar mill in Kahuku, world-famous surfing beaches, Waimea Falls Park, Matsumoto's shave ice in Haleiwa, and the end of the road at Kaena.*

On my first visit to Kahuku fifty-one years ago, in 1941, I watched narrow-gauge steam locomotives pulling harvested sugarcane in from the fields. Black smoke poured from the mill stacks and a low growl sounded from inside as cane was crushed and boiled and spun into sugar. I still remember the wonderful smell of fermenting waste sugar all about the place.

The mill is quiet today. It has begun to fall apart and no longer smells like sugar, but it does contain a restaurant, which makes Kahuku an excellent starting point for our tour of the north shore. Fortucci's at the Mill, which was actually built inside the rusting place, serves breakfast when it opens at 8:30 A.M. On the menu you'll notice Portuguese sausage, Spam, and pork links. Hawaii consumes more Spam per capita than any other state. You must sample the Portuguese sausage made in Hawaii; the "hot" spicy variety is the best of all.

Driving west from Kahuku, you'll come across ponds of shrimp and oysters being raised for the hotel trade—you are in the aquaculture capital of the state. You might be interested in stopping at the roadside stand, where the shrimp for sale are as large as your hand.

In the distance you'll see the Turtle Bay Hilton, surrounded by golf courses on a dramatic peninsula (where I have never seen any turtles). If you didn't stop at Fortucci's for breakfast, try the moderately priced Palm Terrace overlooking the hotel grounds. Remember that there are very few good places to eat on the north shore, so if you're driving around in the middle of the day, stop here for lunch. They serve everything, including local saimin, a Hawaiian noodle soup, and teriyaki.

Soon you come to the north shore beaches along this portion of the highway. Both in the summer months, when the ocean is generally placid and calm, and in the winter—but especially January and February, when waves from northern storms reach Oahu's shore—the beaches are a very dangerous place to be, unless you know how to surf. Island visitors unfamiliar with the ocean should exercise caution. The ocean behaves in unpredictable ways. Considering the vagaries of its personality, even on days when you feel confident it is best to keep your distance, avoiding exposed places. Approached with care, the ocean will provide you with much pleasure and excitement.

North shore surfing

On the north shore the sheer size of the surf is danger-ous, even for the experienced surfer. When the winter waves are cresting at thirty feet and up, it's best to be just looking. Any surfing here in the winter waves should be done by experts.

Another warning to newcomers has to do with the sun. Much of the time the sun in Hawaii is straight overhead, and it is never at an angle lower than forty-five degrees. Also, the air is clear, as you may have noticed, so solar radiation pene-trates directly to your skin. Use a good sunblock, and don't expose yourself for too long a time until a tan is evident.

Most of the well-known surfing areas are signed, although some are not. You can spot the popular places by the number of cars parked along the road. If no parking places remain, the surf is up! The north coast is unprotected by reef, so waves pound in directly on shore, sometimes eroding much of it away. The surfing season runs from October through April, and surfers travel here from all over the globe. Join the crowd—there is always room for spectators on the beach.

The first place of note is Velzyland, off Kaunala, a surfing break with no beach, only rock and reef. The famous Sunset Beach, Paumalu, is next, with some of the most spectacular waves on the island. Ehukai cannot be seen from the high-way, but it is a favored spot from which to watch surfers surfing the renowned Pupukea and Pipeline surfing breaks, which are sometimes referred to as the Banzai Pipeline.

In ancient days the Sunset Beach surf was called Pau-malu, and even back then the place had a reputation for fierce surf. When the chief of Kauai came to Oahu to surf the giant waves at Paumalu, the legendary Bird Maiden saw him and immediately fell in love with him. She sent her messengers to give him an orange lehua lei and guide him to her cave, where he was captivated by her love. The chief stayed a long time until he heard the high surf one day and longed to ride the waves again.

24

The Bird Maiden allowed him to return to the surf if he vowed never to kiss another woman, but after surfing all day, he made love to a beautiful Oahu girl who rode with him on the last wave and then placed an ilima lei upon him. The Bird Maiden's messengers saw the chief break his vow and told her what had happened. When she realized that the chief would never return to Kauai, she turned him into stone, and he remains a rock today on the hill above Sunset, watching the high surf at Paumalu.

I've taken all my children into the ocean at Pupukea Beach Park, in the area called Shark's Cove. In the summer it is great to climb on the rocks and wait for waves to splash in. In the winter it's best not to go near the place. High up on the *pali* behind, in one of the homes at the far end, James Michener lived for a year with his staff while researching his novel *Hawaii*.

Take the Pupukea Road at the supermarket parking lot up the hill, turning right onto the entrance road to Puu o Mahuka Heiau Park. In one of the largest partially restored *heiaus* (shrines) on Oahu, walk to the *makai* (seaward) stone wall for a great view of Waimea Bay and Beach, where the largest surfing waves in the world reach shore. In the winter this area is often battered by murderous, towering waves. Occasional fifty-foot monsters throw spray as far as the highway and make the ground tremble as they break. In the summer the bay is placid, like a lake, and the county park invites families from across the island in urban Honolulu for a day of fun at the beach. The park has daily, year-round lifeguard service. A good rule to remember: Swim in the summer, sunbathe in the winter.

Across the highway from the beach you'll find the entrance to Waimea Falls Park, a Hawaiian arboretum, historical park, and tropical preserve of 1,800 acres crisscrossed with hiking trails and archaeological ruins. (The park charges admission.) One parcel of particular interest features Hawaiian species. For those who prefer not to walk, there is a tram to Waimea Falls, but the park's vast collection of birds and plants can only be fully appreciated on foot. Come to this garden to picnic, swim, or wander about at your leisure.

Beyond Waimea there are more beaches: Kapaeloa, Chun's Reef, Laniakea, and Papailoa. If the cars are lined up along the highway, there is surfing at Kapaeloa, but otherwise in the summer there is only sunbathing, snorkling, and sometimes board surfing.

Before Haleiwa, after the beach homes end, you'll find an interesting but little-known historical site. On the right, on the flat stretch covered with hale koa bushes, there used to be an unpaved, emergency military airstrip. When Pearl Harbor was bombed on the morning of December 7, 1941, the Curtis fighters hidden here took off to fight the enemy aircraft, shooting down two Zeros, the only planes shot down by Americans on that fateful day.

Haleiwa Beach Park follows along the cove entering Haleiwa Bay. Across the bay is Alii Beach, where the north shore sand continues on—all the way to Kaena. Kamehameha Highway crosses a double-rainbow-shaped bridge into the town of Haleiwa (a new highway in the cane field bypasses this bridge, but it is a dull road). The old way is the best way to enter this clapboard plantation town, whose inhabitants comprise transient surfers, counterculturists, and a few local Oriental remainders from the old days. Haleiwa combines with stylish nonchalance the newest shopping centers and the oldest storefronts, and has established itself as the "in" place on the north shore. No city planner of any consequence has ever worked in Haleiwa. It is a historical and architectural jumble and worth all the time you can spare.

Across from the Kealiiokamalu Church, which contains a clock given to the congregation by Queen Liliuokalani in 1832, while Hawaii was still a kingdom, is Matsumoto's shave-ice emporium. No visit to Haleiwa is complete without a taste of the best shave ice in Hawaii. I have never been to Matsumoto's shop when there wasn't a line, even when I first showed up fifty years ago. At that time Matsumoto's was still a grocery store. Today the shelves are empty, but against the back wall his Japanese-made shave-ice machine still produces the treat that everyone from Hawaii raves about.

Not to be confused with the mainland "snow cone," shave ice is better by far, unique to Hawaii. It comes in eleven flavors and three combinations. If you like, you can start out with ice cream or sweet beans in the bottom of your paper cup. Order by color if you want to sound local—"red" means strawberry. Order a "rainbow" if you want a little of everything. Sit outside the shop on the benches provided and drip gleefully all over the pavement.

Back on the corner, past Chun's Market, is the Chart House Restaurant (good teriyaki cheeseburger), site of the grand old Haleiwa Hotel, built in 1899 by Dillingham's Oahu Railroad & Land Company, then carrying sugar and passengers from Honolulu to Kahuku. Haleiwa was a favorite honeymoon stop for newlyweds from Honolulu. Some took the train to Haleiwa just for a weekend overnight. It was *the* place to stay, with a Japanese bridge leading to the beach and bathhouse, long before the yacht harbor and other intrusions. And it was only a short walk up to Matsumoto's place for dessert.

The Haleiwa Hotel is gone now, but the town has plenty to offer. There's dinner if you stay long enough and breakfast if you arrive early. Try Jameson's by the Sea for lunch or dinner—look for a table upstairs. Island Images sells limited-edition prints in the old adobe-colored building with the tile roof, once the north shore branch of First Hawaiian Bank.

(This was the second bank robbed in Hawaii. The first was on Maui.)

Wend your way westward along the shore road, past residences old and new, past cane fields and schools, to the town of Waialua, with its operating sugar mill. Continue past the polo fields and on toward Dillingham Airfield, another World War II facility, this one still in use.

Glider rides are popular here, along with rides in piston-powered biplanes, parachuting, and helicopter sight-seeing trips. General aviation pilots often fly to Dillingham from Honolulu for a day at Mokuleia Beach. I've flown out myself, parked at the end of the runway, and walked to the beach for the weekend. The beach is not very good for swimming, but it's never crowded. Unofficial camping along the beachfront is quite common.

Not too far beyond Mokuleia, on the way to Kaena Point, the paved road gives out and driving becomes rough. Keep going as far as your car is able, but it's best to stop and walk when you feel your car is chewing up the ground too much. Four-wheel drives can make it, but they are ripping up the place terribly, and that's just not the way to treat a nature reserve like Kaena. The walk out to the point is several miles on a very rugged track, if you have the time and the boots. I've done it and recommend it highly.

There are no beaches at Kaena Point, on either side. You're here to experience the raw beauty of rugged lava meeting a turbulent sea at the end of the island. It is said that the highest waves in Hawaii reach shore here, averaging thirty to forty feet, with freak waves even higher. As far as I know, no one has ever tried to ride a surfboard out here. It's no place even to go wading. At the right time—mostly in the summer, occasionally in the winter—you will find Kaena a wonderful place to witness the might and majesty of the sea.

In the Area

All numbers are within area code 808.

Fortucci's at the Mill: 293-1061
Chart House Restaurant, Haleiwa: 637-8005
Jameson's by the Sea: 637-4336

5 ~

Oahu's South Shore:

Hanauma-Waimanalo-Nuuanu Pali

How to get there: From Honolulu, follow State 72 (Kalanianaole Highway) to Koko Crater, Hanauma Bay, Makapuu Point, Waimanalo Beach, and Waimanalo. About two miles outside Waimanalo, State 72 joins State 61. At the junction of State 83 and State 61, bear left to stay on 61. Go through the tunnel and follow signs for Nuuanu Pali Lookout.

Highlights: *Hanauma Bay and the nation's first underwater marine preserve; Halona Blow Hole; body surfing at Sandy Beach; Makapuu Point and a panoramic view of Oahu's windward coast; incomparable Nuuanu Pali Lookout.*

Where you leave the dense residential area of south Oahu on Kalanianaole Highway (State 72) and begin driving up the slope of Koko Crater, you are passing through one of the single largest developed areas on the island: Hawaii Kai, a multimillion-dollar personal project of famed industrialist Henry Kaiser. He built his own mansion on the Koko Head shore and spent the last years of his life mostly building homes and condos in Hawaii Kai and managing a vast industrial empire from his business office in Waikiki, in the hotel he built, now the Hilton Hawaiian Village. All the construction equipment used in his projects was painted pink. So was his sailing catamaran at Waikiki.

The view of Hanauma Bay from the parking area entrance reveals old volcanic crater walls that almost encircle a turquoise bay filled with the jagged shapes of living coral. On a clear day Molokai Island can be seen on the horizon, but most visitors focus their attention on the spectacular view below—the first protected marine preserve in the nation and another of the prettiest beaches in Hawaii, edging a wonderful bay of coral under calm water. Adults and children wander about on the coral as if walking on water, occasionally stopping to marvel at the underwater life teeming at their feet. Others with snorkel gear float gently on the water observing schools of fish gathering for food and attention. It is a marvelous experience.

The swimming and snorkeling here are beyond compare. Even a stroll along the bay rim beyond the ends of the beach is a small-scale adventure. To the left, you'll find the "Toilet Bowl," where incoming waves flush out the rocky pool.

Much of Elvis Presley's movie *Blue Hawaii* was filmed here. The beach was also seen in *From Here To Eternity*. The bay is very popular with local people, so plan your visit for a weekday, extra-early in the morning, if you expect to find any parking space.

Continuing on around Koko Head, past many small, inviting coves, you soon reach Halona Blow Hole. Try out one of the coves first. Climb down and imagine one of these tiny beaches as your own private domain. I've done this on many occasions.

It is hard to know whether the blow hole will be performing on the day you arrive to see it, for the parking lot will inevitably be crowded with sightseers wondering the same

31

Blow Hole Beach on the south shore

thing. I can only suggest you hang around a bit. Spend some time people-watching in the small beach cove on your right.

To the east you can see the sweep of Sandy Beach, a popular place for body surfing. On most days the surf exhibits an unusual tendency, which poor swimmers should be aware of. The outgoing wave pulls surfers out into the breaking surf but suddenly drops them into the incoming wave, which then carries them back up the beach. In the better summer weather it is practically impossible to drown at this beach. I've come here often.

Continuing on past the golf course that Kaiser built, and up the grade ahead, you will find Makapuu Point, presenting a grand panoramic view of windward Oahu. Look for Rabbit Island just offshore. Makapuu Beach is another excellent body-surfing beach. The waves here roll in much bigger than at Sandy Beach, but they don't have the nice characteristic of holding you back from the sea after they break. Board surfing is not permitted here, so at least the body surfer need not keep checking for loose boards. Huge swells often generate the surf here, waves that can slam the novice into the rocky shore or down into the sand. Ambulances carry body surfers away with broken backs and necks with disturbing regularity. If you jump in on a stormy day, beware.

Inland of our road is Sea Life Park, a marine attraction featuring performing dolphins, whales, sharks, stingrays, and other marine life, similar to marine exhibits on the mainland. The park allows you to see the bird and marine life of Hawaii close up and to feed the sea animals. Dolphins in leis and false killer whales perform outdoors in a pool with a replica of the whaling ship *Essex*.

The top edge of the high *pali* behind Sea Life Park is a favorite launching pad for hang-gliding enthusiasts, who drive up a narrow access road from the Hawaii Kai area. On lazy summer days when thermal updrafts are fully functioning, the gliders will be performing at their best and may be in the air for several hours at a time, soaring out over the ocean and back toward the *pali*, before coming in for a landing on the beach below. Watch for them.

The road continues along the shore into the Waimanalo Hawaiian community, traveling between soft sand beach parks and individual homes of every style. *Mauka* (inland), the Koolau Range, an impressive array of fluted green cliffs averaging 3,000 feet in height, dominates the view. The mountains slope gently down into Honolulu on the other side, but over here they rise in nearly vertical ranks that extend for miles, interrupted only occasionally by small valleys. The precipitous mountains are at their best in changing weather, in the dance of light and shade.

If you are traveling on a Sunday, stop at the corner grocery store and ask where the Hawaiian Trail and Mountain Club clubhouse is located. The clubhouse makes a good place to change, if you wish, for a windward swim. It was built in 1915 and for many years was the only structure in this area of Waimanalo, an old sugar plantation now growing papayas and bananas.

Outside of town, as the road winds northward, you arrive at Olomana Peak, a favorite hiking destination of mine over the years. The first peak is much easier to climb than it looks. I've often eaten lunch on top with other hiking friends who have taken on the rock scramble.

Keep left at the road junctions to Kailua and Kaneohe and take the highway to Honolulu up and through the *pali* tunnel. After exiting continue on to the right turn, which takes you over the old *pali* road, through ferns and vines, up to the Nuuanu Pali Lookout. Don't miss this view, described by many as Oahu's finest. Kamehameha I is said to have pushed his opponents over the *pali* from this point when he conquered Oahu in 1795.

Spend some time here and admire the magnificent view, because I helped preserve it. In the early 1960s, the Castle Ranch group, which owned all the land below the *pali*, submitted plans for a subdivision that would have completely covered this property. All the engineering was done, streets were named, and water and sewage systems designed. In 1960 I was appointed a Hawaii state land use commissioner by Governor Burns, for whom I had campaigned. The governor created the commission, which was charged with zoning all the land in the state, in part to preserve scenic land such as the *pali* view. I assigned top priority to stopping the proposed subdivision and was able to convince the other commissioners to vote unanimously to zone all the land below the *pali* as "conservation" land, making it impossible for the landowners to obtain county approval and building permits for the project. The subdivision was abandoned. Eventually the county acquired the land and built their golf courses. The Nuuanu Pali view, extending from Makapuu Point to the far shore of Kaneohe Bay, was saved for residents and visitors to appreciate, forever. The land is still zoned "conservation," and it is still beautiful.

In the Area

All numbers are within area code 808.

Sea Life Park: 259-7933

6 ~

Central Oahu:

Wahiawa-Schofield Barracks-Kolekole-KuniaRoad-Waipahu

How to get there: From Honolulu, take I-H1 to Pearl City and head north on I-H2 to Wahiawa. Your tour of central Oahu begins there.

Highlights: *The pineapple fields of the high central Oahu plateau; sacred birthing stones at Kukaniloho; a drive through Schofield Barracks to Kolekole Pass overlooking Lualualei Valley and the Waianae Range, a sweeping view of Pearl Harbor and Honolulu.*

Central Oahu is known chiefly for its military installations. We'll begin our drive in Wahiawa, which sits on the 1,000-foot-high Leilehua Plateau in the middle of the island. The military presence is everywhere—Schofield Barracks, Wheeler Field, and other installations, many far underground, built during World War II when it was expected that the Japanese would return to invade Oahu.

Dillingham's railroad had been running trains from downtown Honolulu to Wahiawa for many years. The OR&L railroad depot was located in the central part of town, east of the highway on North Cane Street. A few of the Wild West

36

storefronts (with balconies, in some cases) can still be seen, some dating as far back as 1910.

It was in this area that Jim Dole grew his first pineapples, which were much larger than the Central American specimens from which his plants were bred. The cannery staff invented a fast way to peel and core the fruit, while Dole continued to develop pineapple of the best size for canning— something no one had thought of doing before. His success made possible the pineapple-canning industry in Hawaii.

Today it is relatively easy to pick your own ripe pineapples from the fields (they are by far the sweetest), but thirty years ago the plantations were very wary of strangers wandering about. All strangers were suspected of being foreign agents trying to steal Dole's young plants so that their countries could capture the market for pineapples. Now the Dole company grows its own fruit overseas at half the cost of its Hawaiian operations.

Farther out on the highway north of Wahiawa is a Dole Pineapple Pavilion, where you can enjoy free pineapple juice and purchase fresh pineapple to take home. On your return to Wahiawa, look for the sample patch of pineapple plants from the tropics growing at the highway junction. They are labeled to give you an idea of what Dole started out with.

Continuing farther back, take the dirt road opposite Whitmore Avenue to Kukaniloho, a cluster of sacred stones under eucalyptus and coconut palms. These are the birthing stones of Hawaiian royalty. *Alii* gave birth here with great ceremony, to the accompaniment of nose flutes, chants, drums, and offerings. Kukaniloho has been a sacred place since the twelfth century and plays an important role in Hawaiian mythology, but use of the site declined and eventually stopped following the arrival of the Europeans.

Harvesting pineapples

Returning to the paved road, drive north, bearing left at all junctions, until you reach the main entrance to Schofield Barracks, across from Kemoo Farms Restaurant. Should you wish to join military friends for a drink and dinner, this is the place to go.

Pull into the Macomb entrance to Schofield, home of the 25th Infantry Division, and ask the guard for directions to Kolekole Pass. You will undoubtedly get lost (as I have many times), but there is lots to see in the Barracks area, so don't worry. You are at the heart of the film *From Here to Eternity*. Stop in at the Tropics Lightning Museum, which features the battle records of the Schofield soldiers. On that "day of infamy" when the Japanese attacked Pearl Harbor, they dropped a few bombs here after buzzing through Kolekole notch.

There's another sentry just before Kolekole Pass. Ask the guard for permission to drive to the observation point. He will generally say yes. If he is uncooperative on the day you arrive, park and walk. Also try the footpath that begins before the gate and leads up the hill near the cross. Old-timers say the rock above the parking area represents Kolekole, the female guardian of the pass.

The view from Kolekole in both directions is very impressive. The Waianae Range drops away suddenly, and you feel as if you were flying. The vast Lualualei Valley (a naval ammunition storage area) opens up to Oahu's west coast. The military road traveling down into Lualualei is a spectacular drive but is seldom open to the public. Ask anyway. There might be an open day on their schedule.

Driving back through Schofield, turn right onto Kunia Road, traveling south past Wheeler Field. Shortly the road goes downhill into a gulch. On the right is the entrance to a three-story, underground aircraft-assembly and maintenance facility built early during World War II beneath the pineapple field. Ready to fly, fighters would exit directly onto a ramp crossing the highway that led to a paved airstrip in the bottom of the gulch. Underground fuel supplies and radio communications supported the facility. Today the site belongs to the Navy.

On my drives into central Oahu I have always returned to downtown Honolulu via Kunia Road, because about a third of the way back, on the gentle downward slope, the entire western shore on both sides of Pearl Harbor opens up to view. Often in the late afternoon a rainbow will drift *makai* (seaward) from the perpetually green mountains. Slow down along the road, pull off into a pineapple field, and stop to absorb. If it's late in the afternoon, wait for the sun to set.

The rainbow is mostly "liquid sunshine," a misty drizzle falling lazily from broken cumulus clouds blowing with the trade winds as they break away from clinging hills. When the city forgets to pick up after itself, a drifting night rain washes the dust away.

Honolulu is basic green, blue, and white—the colors of the mountains, the sea, and the sky. The space surrounding the green hills is blue, delineated by the highest ridge and softened by *mauka* (landward) showers moving slowly toward the city. The rain falls from white cumulus clouds that break away from the mountaintops in long clusters, clinging briefly to the hills before letting go and bringing to the city moisture, shade, and coolness. Hawaii is famous for the trade winds that create this daily weather pattern and make meteorologists quite unnecessary.

White buildings dominate the skyline, hugging the surf line like a crown-flower lei that has been thrown into the sea and, having floated back to shore, is caught in the ceaseless sweep of waves upon the land. All this can be seen from Kunia.

In the Area

All numbers are within area code 808.

Dole Pineapple Plantation Visitors' Center: 621-8408
Kemo's Farm Restaurant: 621-8481
Schofield Barracks, 25th Infantry: 471-7110

7 ~

Molokai's Halawa Valley:

Kaunakakai-Waialua-Halawa

How to get there: From Kaunakakai, drive east on State 450.

Highlights: *The sleepy town of Kaunakakai and hot bread fresh from the oven at night; Kakahaia National Wildlife Refuge; Mapulehu Valley; ironwood, koa, eucalyptus, kukui, red guava, Surinam cherry, and sour Java plum trees; Halawa Valley and Moaula waterfall.*

On Molokai, the Pau Hana Inn is the place to stay. It's almost as old as Kaunakakai, and it's the one place on the island where everyone has been at one time or another. Hanging out is the pastime at the Pau Hana Inn. (*Pau hana* translates loosely as "après work.") The food and drinks aren't bad either, and unlike the rest of Hawaii, the prices are reasonable.

You know when it's Saturday in Kaunakakai, because the main street becomes crowded. Shoppers take over the street as if they were in a shopping center. Kaunakakai has the feel of a one-horse town. Not much has changed here in the last fifty years. There are still benches on the street where locals sit to watch other locals. Molokai has always been something of a backwater, and residents seem to like it that way. They just don't operate like people in Honolulu.

I remember one late afternoon when I was photographing a *hukilau* (seiner) along the shore. When the crew finished bringing in the loaded net, they gave me a nice-size fish. I stopped at the Midnight Inn on my way back to town and asked them if they could broil it for me. My dinner was soon served—at the lowest price on the menu.

On my last visit I was told how to get a late-night loaf of hot bread at Kanemitsu's Bakery & Coffee Shop, on the main street, after closing time. When you drive into Kaunakakai, follow the smell of baking bread. This will lead you to the alley between Imamura's place and the Sight & Sound shop. Find the back door of the bakery. Knock and ask for a loaf of hot bread, sliced in half and loaded with butter, cream cheese, or cinnamon. The choices are French raisin, cheese, white, onion-cheese, brown, and wheat, or whatever happens to be coming out of the oven just then. Is this possible anywhere else?

As you drive south from Kaunakakai, watch for Kawela hillside subdivision, turn in there, and drive to the top for a great view of the coconut-fringed shore, Kanoa Fish Pond, and the white surf line along the reef. At the top of this subdivision you are near Kawela battlefield, an important Molokai historical site. High on an almost inaccessible ridge in the middle of Kawela Gulch is a fortress-*heiau*, marking where Kamehameha I fought for possession of Molokai. Tradition holds it to be a place of refuge where those about to be captured or slain in battle could find sanctuary.

Kamehameha I (or the Great) was born on the Big Island in about 1760 and raised in Waipio Valley. After Captain Cook's visit to Hawaii, Kamehameha decided to subdue the Big Island's feuding chiefs and establish himself as ruler. In

1791, with the help of European cannon, he won a decisive battle and took control of the island. His ultimate goal was to create a single kingdom incorporating all the islands.

His first battle on the outer islands took place in east Maui, in the Hana area, the birthplace of his favorite wife, Kaahumanu. One by one he conquered all the islands: Maui, Molokai, Lanai, and Oahu, where his famous final battle was fought at Nuuanu Pali. By 1795 Kamehameha ruled all the major islands except Kauai, where his invasion fleet of outrigger canoes was turned back by a storm.

Kamehameha abolished human sacrifice but otherwise made few liberal concessions during his autocratic reign and is remembered chiefly for bloodying streams and beaches in island battles. During his twenty-four years as king, the Hawaiian population plunged from an estimated 300,000 to about 135,000. Why this Hawaiian Napoleon is so honored today remains a mystery to many.

Kamehameha died in 1819, in his sixties, and his body was hidden in a secret place near Kailua Kona so that others could not draw magical power from his bones. He was succeeded by four other Kamehamehas. By 1893 the dynasty had ended.

You'll find ancient Hawaiian fish ponds along the shore for many miles. At one time there were sixty-two ponds, all stocked with fish, with grills set in ocean-side gates to keep predators out and mature fish in—a type of aquaculture unique to the islands. On some of the ponds, particularly in the Kakahaia National Wildlife Refuge, you can see the endangered Hawaiian stilt, moorhen, Hawaiian duck, and black-crowned night heron.

A bit farther on, at Kawalo, is St. Joseph's Church, one of several community churches built in 1876 by Father Damien before he entered Kalaupapa leper settlement. The church was one of the first structures in the area to be built of wood. So impressed were the local residents that they abandoned their traditional thatch construction and switched to the new material.

Driving along the only shore road on Molokai, we pass through many ancient, named *ahupuaas*, parcels of land divided by early chiefs into wedge-shaped pieces extending from the sea to the mountain summits. No names appear on road markers at present, but during the months ahead local residents plan to put these names up so that visitors will have a better sense of where they are on the island.

A mile farther on, a small plaque beside the highway at Keawenui marks the spot where in 1927 pilot Ernest Smith and navigator Emory Bronte crashed their plane, which had run out of gas, into scrubby kiawe trees, ending the first civilian flight from California to Hawaii. The kiawe they crashed into were cut down and turned into charcoal in 1955, before historical sites were considered worth saving.

At the end of a manicured lawn at Kaluaaha, on the *mauka* (inland) side of the road, are the ruins of the first church on Molokai, built in 1844 by the Reverend Hitchcock, the first missionary.

There are several places to stay along the way. The first is Hotel Molokai, built in an unusual architectural style that seems quite appropriate to the island. The rooms have no telephones or televisions. A nice place to go to escape civilization. Farther down the road are the Alii Park condos, referred to as "the old rice patch" by locals, and the Wavecrest condos, both with overnight rooms.

It was at Hotel Molokai that I first met Richard Marks, who runs the guided auto tour of the leper colony in Kalaupapa.

45

He invited me to fly in and said he would arrange for me to stay overnight in his lighthouse guest house. It was something of a shock for me to learn that he himself had been afflicted with leprosy.

Kalaupapa was a scene of tragedy and heartbreak in the latter half of the nineteenth century, when those afflicted with leprosy were actually thrown ashore on the Kalaupapa Peninsula to die of their disease. The cliffs and the ocean kept these unfortunate people isolated from the rest of the world until Father Damien (Joseph De Veuster) arrived in 1873. This Belgian priest spent the next sixteen years—for the first ten of which he worked entirely alone—trying to improve sanitation, housing, and the food supply for the residents of the colony. After contracting leprosy himself, Father Damien refused treatment in order to remain with his flock and died of the disease in 1889.

All but children under the age of sixteen can now visit Kalaupapa and meet with the patients with arrested disease, which is not communicable. The patients are free to leave, but they have chosen to live out their lives in the place to which their ancestors were banished years ago, without shelter or provisions. The town is noted for its large number of pet dogs, who receive the attention and affection that would normally have been lavished on children. There are no residents of child-bearing age.

I remember camping in Mapulehu Valley in preparation for a tough, all-day hike up and over the island to Wailau Valley, past the highest mountain peak on Molokai. On one visit we found the Mapulehu water tank full when we arrived at the end of a hot day, so we floated our watermelon in the tank, anticipating a cold treat for dessert. After our group had spent the afternoon bathing and drawing cooking water from the tank, we reached in for the melon, only to find that it had sunk halfway down the tank. We had used most of the water.

I held our thinnest camper by the feet, lowering him in to withdraw our melon.

Mapalehu Valley occupies an important place in Molokai history. At the head of the valley, by the Wailau Trail, is the island's largest and possibly oldest *heiau* (shrine), Iliiliopae, almost 1,000 feet long. According to several historians, the entire valley was once a place of refuge and asylum. The *heiau* was dedicated to the highest gods worshipped throughout the islands and staffed by resident priests. It was near here that Kamehameha lived when he visited Molokai.

Islander Philip Spalding III tells a story about the *heiau*. According to legend, an evil high chief and his followers sacrificed nine sons of a local resident at one time. The man appealed for justice to the fearsome shark god of Molokai's northern coast, and a rainstorm and flood promptly cleansed the temple, sweeping the evildoers out to sea, where they were eaten by sharks. They became sacrifices to their own gods in retribution for the crime they had committed.

Across the road from Mapulehu Valley, in the state's largest mango orchard, the Mapulehu wagon ride departs for the *heiau* and other parts of the valley. The ride lasts a couple of hours and is great fun. Mapulehu, many years ago, was the location of the largest commercial lime grove in the islands, and limes grown in Molokai backyards are still highly prized. Grapes grew abundantly here at one time, and a Hawaiian wine industry was envisioned.

People in passing cars are always waving. Wave back. It's quiet on the road because people don't honk their horns. Here and there a new home on the hillside is under construction where the original Hawaiian owners have sold a portion of their land and sent kids on to college. Others have stayed, mostly around the bays, earning salaries or receiving county relief instead of subsisting on wet-land agriculture. At Honouliwai Bay a single stone fish trap survives from the old days

Bird of paradise

when the community gathered food from the sea. Some Hawaiian families still grow a little taro, maintaining continuity with the past. Young Hawaiians drop by to learn the old ways before they leave for Honolulu and jobs.

The Ah Ping store, on the shore road near Pukoo, is all boarded up. Note the price of gas on the abandoned gas pump. Ah Ping was a samurai in Japan who sailed to Hawaii under a sugar contract and eventually ended up as manager of a sugar company on Maui. In his retirement he became the owner of a general store on Molokai. His life story would require another book.

The reef gets closer and closer to the shore as we travel on, nearly touching the rocky shore along the Pailolo Channel between Molokai and Maui. The shallows reveal the coral's muted colors through clear water. At Honouliwai Point, fires are set as a beacon for late-returning fishermen. The people sitting on the rocks are net fishermen looking for fish. When they see fish, they throw their nets in. People picking in the rocks are looking for opihi, a good-eating shellfish that makes excellent soup.

As you cross Waialua Stream bridge, look up to the right at the old taro planter's house, a board-and-batten structure built in the 1920s. I remember staying there for a week. The sloping yard, fenced to keep cattle out, ends at a beach shaded by huge false kamani trees. We could see the edge of the reef and Turtle Island (Mokoniki) offshore, with Maui Island in the distance. Although taro was no longer being grown along the road and up in the narrow valley, a stay in the house was a wonderful island experience nonetheless. Living out here on Molokai, far from everything—without gas, without electricity, without television, without telephone —we were on our own. Sometimes running water would come to the kitchen through a pipe from the *auwai* (water ditch) up behind the house. Sometimes not. We cooked on propane. Hissing Coleman gas lanterns provided light. We lived a completely different lifestyle.

Posted on the kitchen wall were the usual typewritten instructions for renters, plus several comments found only at Waialua: "If the house catches fire, gather your valuables and go outside. The fire department will not arrive in time to do any good." And then at the end: "The Molokai police never come this far except in case of murder."

Gordon Morse, a Molokai friend who has also stayed in the taro planter's house, has described a Waialua night:

The shore is shadowed early from mountains behind, so the spectacle before you as sunset nears is the lushness of west Maui. The greenery turns bluish, then purple as the channeled ocean seems to shrink and the island looms larger in the twilight. The lights of high-rise tourism at Kaanapali twinkle and an occasional car's headlights flash around a curve. A Molokai night is incredibly silent. With no radio, TV, or traffic, with even the volume on the surf turned down, the quiet comes on like an invisible fog. You lie in bed and wonder about that soft pounding noise, only to realize it's your own heart beating.

The road now turns inland and winds uphill to the Puu o Hoku (Hill of the Stars) Ranch. As the road nears the summit, a stone wall on the left and a gate identify the edge of a grass airfield with an uphill runway. The ranch at one time welcomed rich hunters, who roamed the ranchlands for deer. As the road snakes through ranch buildings, a kukui tree grove can be seen far on the right—Ka Ulu Kukui o Lanikaula, the most sacred kukui grove in Hawaii and a highly venerated place for Molokai.

You drive through a marvelous forest as you near Halawa: ironwood trees, native koa, eucalyptus, kukui, wild Christmas berry, red guava, Surinam cherries, and the sour Java plum. At Lamaloa Head, which overlooks the oldest recorded inhabited site on Molokai, dating from 650 A.D., you'll get your first view of Halawa.

Halawa was well populated before a tsunami wave over thirty feet high swept through in 1946, wiping out taro patches and homes covering the valley entrance. Broad Halawa Stream, which once filled seventy-seven separate taro patches, still winds through the valley, but now fills only an isolated ditch before it reaches the ocean. Two hundred years ago there were an estimated 1,023 individually engineered taro patches. Only traces of them remain today.

50

Halawa Valley is considered one of the most scenic Hawaiian valleys, like Hanalei on Kauai, Kahana on Oahu, and Waipio on Hawaii Island, but unlike these other valleys, Halawa has been inhabited continuously since the Polynesians first settled the islands. Only two other places in Hawaii reveal evidence of earlier occupation: South Point on Hawaii Island and the Bellows Field shore on Oahu.

The pavement ends just past the old school site, shortly before you reach the shore. A dirt road to the left enters into Dupree Dudoit's lot. For $5, Dudoit, a Halawa old-timer, offers you a secure parking place in his yard while you hike up the valley. Bananas and sodas await you on your return. Dudoit told me that the rental car agency charges $25 to bring a replacement key if you lose yours. If you park in his yard he will drive you to the airport free—one of the better deals in the islands. It seems that many car keys are lost in Halawa Valley.

The first building you reach as you walk up the valley is the freshly painted, green Protestant church, still in use and always open. People do live and farm in the valley; you will pass their homes on the way to Moaula waterfall, a round trip of several hours, including stream crossings and other adventures. You will probably get lost and wander around a bit. Bring a lunch in your daypack so you can eat along the way in the jungle. All your efforts will be repaid when you reach your goal. The Moaula pool is fantastic, wide and deep enough for diving, with large boulders to lounge and sunbathe on. A perfect spot for lovers.

If you are planning on swimming at Moaula, local residents say you must first drop a single ti leaf in the pool, to appease the giant moo (lizard) living below the falls. If the leaf floats, it's alright to swim. If it sinks, stay out of the water or the moo will be watching for you. On a day when the falls are roaring full and the pool is turbulent, the leaf will sink. Don't go in.

51

In my book *Maui No Ka Oi*, I wrote: "The road to Halawa Valley must never be paved. This valley is a treasure and it will remain a place of escape . . . as long as the road stays rough." The road has been paved, but this valley is still a treasure—for now.

In the Area

All numbers are within area code 808.

Pau Hana Inn: 553-5342

Kanemitsu's Bakery and Coffee Shop: 553-5855

Hotel Molokai: 553-5347

Mapulehu wagon rides: 558-8380

8 ~

Maui's

Hana

Road:

Paia-Kailua-
Keanae-Hana

How to get there: From Paia, head north to the junction of State 36, which becomes State 360, the famous Hana Highway.

Highlights: *The old plantation town of Paia, Mama's Fish House, waterfalls at every turn, a jungle of tropical trees and flowers, the vanishing village of Nahiku, Waianapanapa State Park, a nostalgic ride on the Hana Highway.*

The road to Hana is to a certain extent a dream, an idea, in the minds of those who have never been there and want to visit this strange point in east Maui, on the far side of great Haleakala. The Hana Highway is described so often in travel guides and brochures that prospective travelers hardly know how to appreciate it when they finally find themselves on it. This road is not a way to get anywhere. It is a destination in itself.

But Paia is as good a place to start as any. Paia, like Hana, is an old plantation town, built by plantation people. The town's population has changed completely, from Oriental in plantation days to *haoles* (whites) today. Perhaps you were wondering where all the young people from the sixties went. They are in Paia, and they're the same age, wearing the same clothes, and listening to the same music. The only difference is that the current group seems to consist mostly of wind-surfers, for one of the world's premier windsurfing areas is only a mile or so down the road at Hookipa, on the way to Hana. The Paia sugar mill is just above town, still crushing sugar, but workers no longer live in the plantation camps that once surrounded the town. The camps have disappeared along with Paia's former inhabitants.

My last visit to Paia was a strange experience compared with the stop I made here in 1944 on my first trip to Hana. In 1993 there was not a single Oriental on the street—everyone was a *haole*. The only general stores I could find that sugar workers would have felt comfortable patronizing were the Nagata and Horiguchi Markets. Everything else was new—a T-shirt factory, Paia Video, The Wine Corner, Hana-Hou Gallery, Nature's Nectar, Mint Stop, Da Maui Gecko Factory, windsurfer shops, and Peach's & Crumble Cafe & Bakery, which I plan to try on my next visit. It's got to be good with a name like that.

Not too far past Paia is one of the best restaurants on Maui, Mama's Fish House. Look for the fancy old station wagon out front. Hookipa is around the corner from Mama's —in fact you can watch the windsurfing action as you enjoy your meal. The best view of the flock of brightly colored sailboards, however, is from the highest parking area above the beach.

The only transportation to Hana during the war years when I first traveled the road was Redo's bread and mail truck. Piled high in the stake truck, in addition to crates of bread, were live chickens, a couple of pigs, two fifty-gallon barrels of kerosene, and sacks of potatoes, onions, and lettuce for Hasegawa's General Store in Hana and places on the way. I sat on top of it all, on a bag of onions.

Redo stopped everywhere along the then unpaved Hana Road—at Kailua, Keanae, Wailua, Nahiku, and several unnamed places in the middle of nowhere—to greet a customer or friend, to pick someone up or drop someone off. The trip was a grand introduction to rural Maui and its life-style. I imagine that the people living along the road think of the old days of Redo's truck with nostalgia.

Long green ridges drop down from Haleakala's summit to the east shore of Maui, meeting the ocean at Keanae and Wailua in a clash of black lava and blue sea. Only the narrow Hana Highway briefly interrupts this descent, cutting through forests of pandanus, bamboo, and exotic flowering trees and twisting in and out of deep gulches. Almost every turn reveals a waterfall, and there are more than 100 turns in the fifty miles between Paia and Hana. The roadside begins in sugarcane and pineapple, which yield to breadfruit, koa, kukui, ohia, paperbark, mango, guava, tangled hau, and giant 'ape leaves, all scented with wild ginger and accented by flowers of every color.

Before the road was built, the natives in Hana hiked a trail from east Maui to central Maui that went over and through Haleakala. As you drive into dense forests of bamboo, under a canopy of uluhe fern intermingled with native and non-native trees, palms, ferns, and vines, you realize that this is no place to try to walk cross-country.

Hau thickets, their blossoms slowly turning from bright yellow when they open in the morning to a deep brown when they die in the late afternoon, cover entire hillsides, creating a topography of their own and shading the maidenhair fern growing among the cool rocks beneath. In the spring, the mountain apple is covered in puffs of red-tinged blossoms. In early fall, the road is covered with overripe mangoes that have fallen and smashed against the asphalt. Far below the road, cold flows of *aa* (rough) lava plunge into the waves, pushing aside breaking combers as if the lava were still hot from Haleakala's summit.

From high roadside vantage points and parks along the way, you catch glimpses of Keanae and Wailua villages, where Captain Cook anchored and two cultures collided. The geometric patterns of taro patches, the coconut palms, the splayed banana leaves against weather-beaten huts—all are scenes that Captain Cook would recognize.

Where the road makes a sharp bend in the forest before turning off to Keanae, an arboretum has been established, growing every flowering plant you have seen along the way: banks of colorful impatiens, huge 'ape leaves, many varieties of ginger—torch, red, white, and kahili—as well as heliconia, plumeria, and more.

Keanae village lies near sea level on an old flow of *pahoehoe* (smooth lava). From a black pebble beach, villagers launch their frail skiffs and outrigger canoes into the wild surf. The last man pushes the boat free and leaps aboard. The helmsman pulls a knotted rope and the outboard motor churns to life, its roar quickly muffled by the waves as the canoe moves away toward the fishing grounds. Ashore, women pound taro into poi on the shaded lanai of simple homes scattered around a church with coral walls. Over a century old, the church is still in use. The salt-laden winds have weathered the shingled roofs of the buildings, but inside you are likely to find polished floors of island hardwood.

Stop at nearby Wailua, an ethnically diverse community surrounded by taro patches, and visit St. Gabriel's mission with the two bright-red hearts painted above its entrance. When the church builders needed coral blocks and sand to finish construction, the waves providently heaped the

Church at Wailua

needed materials upon the shore in a single night. In gratitude, the residents often drape the shoulders of the life-size Christ outside the church with a flower lei.

Farther south along the road, a miniature state park at Puakea offers two fern-banked pools, each with a misty waterfall. Below the road, the village of Nahiku, almost entirely abandoned, is slowly returning to jungle. The old village landing, where coastal sailing ships once unloaded equipment and supplies used in building the Hana Road and adjacent irrigation ditches, is gradually disappearing.

When Hana was not connected by road to central Maui and the coastal steamer operated on a weekly schedule, Hana-bound travelers who were unwilling to wait for the boat could drive their cars to the road's end at Kailua, ride horseback to Kaumahina ridge, then walk down the switchback trail into Honomanu Valley. Friends would carry them on flatbed taro trucks across the Keanae peninsula to Wailua Cove. By outrigger canoe it was a short ride beyond Wailua to Nahiku landing, where they could borrow a car for the rest of the journey to Hana. Sometimes the trip could be completed in a day. Bad weather could make it last a week or more. Not until 1926 was the road finally connected after years of hard labor.

For many years, until it was paved, the road was little more than a wide mud-and-gravel path. Even after it was paved, mudslides plagued the road. At first the Keanae Chinese store offered overnight rooms to stranded motorists, but later it became the accepted practice for a driver to wait at the mudslide for a car to appear from the opposite direction, then slosh across the intervening gap and offer to exchange cars with the complete stranger on the other side. A handshake would make the temporary trade official, and both parties would agree to meet the next day when the mud had been removed by county work crews, who usually arrived on horseback within a few hours. Recently I was stopped by a small landslide pouring mud across the road, but nowadays there is so much traffic that a group of us, equipped with shovels, were able to clear the mud away by ourselves within a few hours.

Take your time and stop everywhere. There are nature trails and parks along the way, with lots to see and enjoy. It is wise to begin the trip early—be on the road out of Paia by at least 7:00 A.M. so that you can stay ahead of the tourist traffic. Hana Highway is easy to drive if you are not in a hurry. If, for some unaccountable reason, you are in a hurry, drive the road at night so you can spot the headlights of oncoming cars before they reach the curve ahead. Although the road is narrow, it is wide enough for two cars in most places. It just doesn't look it. You'll have to wait for oncoming cars at many one-lane bridges and curves, but consider this an opportunity to look around and enjoy the plants, flowers, and exotic trees.

Shortly after the Hana airport entrance road, about four miles from town, you'll come to the entrance to Waianapanapa State Park, which contains twelve rustic cabins with all-electric kitchens. Beautiful Paialoa Bay, with its black sand beach and black rock shore fringed with green beach naupaka bushes, is part of the park. The beach is noted for its unusual, smooth volcanic pebbles, which are a pleasure to hold and manipulate.

Along the way to Waianapanapa Caves you'll find several historical sites, *heiaus,* and old cemeteries (and lots of mosquitoes). The thick vines lining the path were a sign that the Hawaiian *alii* (royalty) had declared the area *kapu* (forbidden). Cold, clear water runs through the caves. At certain times of the year the water turns red, apparently from infestations of tiny red shrimp, but a local legend offers a different explanation for the phenomenon. A beautiful Hawaiian princess, Popoalaea, fleeing her cruel husband, Kaka'e, hid in the caves. He discovered her there and killed her, and the waters have been turning red periodically ever since.

The abundance of naupaka along the Waianapanapa shore is accounted for by another legend. A beautiful village girl and a handsome *alii* prince fell in love but were forbidden to see each other. To ensure that they obeyed, the two were separated permanently. He was sent to the mountains, she to the shore. When they defied their families by meeting, they were turned into flowers—the naupaka. As you will see as you travel about, naupaka grows both in the mountains and by the sea. Both the mountain and the beach plant bear what appears to be a half-flower, symbolizing the prince and the girl, each yearning for the other.

Hana is continually reinventing itself, embracing people, plants, cultures, and languages and melding them into something called the "island way." The Polynesian village gave way to the sugar town, which became a cow town, which is turning into a resort community. I wish I could drive to Hana again for the first time, but that Hana is gone. It was traveling the road that mattered most, anyway. Even though the Hana Road is now the Hana Highway, that much hasn't changed.

In the Area

All numbers are within area code 808.

Mama's Fish House: 579-8488

Waianapanapu State Park: 243-5354

9 ~

Maui's

Kipahulu

Road:

Hana-Hamoa-Kipahulu-Kaupo

How to get there: From Hana, continue south on State 31.

Highlights: *Sunrise at Hana, Hasegawa's General Store, Hamoa Beach, Oheo Gulch, Kipahulu Valley, Charles Lindbergh's grave.*

Hana is home to the Hotel Hana-Maui, perhaps Hawaii's finest, with accommodations for 100 or so guests, and Hasegawa's General Store, the best and most crowded general store in Hawaii. (For those who have previously visited Hana, the original store burned down and the business has relocated now in the Hana Theater building.) The hotel's main building, including the lobby and dining room, has been completely rebuilt by the new owners, and new management is in charge. The prices are higher, the food is better, and the mai tai's are still selling well.

The town has changed little since I first visited in 1944,

the year that San Francisco industrialist Paul Fagan bought the place and started converting the sugarcane fields to cattle-grazing land. The hotel Fagan built was small and therefore did not disrupt the casual life-style of Hana's residents.

It still rains a lot here. If the sun is going to shine, it will do so in the morning. The afternoon sun is a brief event on this side of Haleakala. Forget photography if the sky is cloudy at dawn, because nothing better will develop in the after-noon. Once, on an assignment to photograph the hotel, I spent an entire week waiting for the sun to come out.

My usual walk begins just beyond the Hana school, across from the ballpark and *makai* of the hotel. A short road starts here at the base of Kauiki Hill, gradually disap-pearing in the high grass near a barbed-wire fence along the adjoining pasture. Climb over the fence into the pasture, head for the shore, and leave your cares behind. The sun sets early in Hana. Haleakala's enormous bulk begins to cast a long seaward shadow early in the afternoon, softening all contours and gradually fusing all colors into the simple black tones of night. Far out at sea, and in the sky overhead, day-time blue lingers long after the scattered lights of Hana are turned on.

Leaving Hana, the highway leads you through pasture-land, past the white Buddhist church on the hill, and on to Puuiki. Here and there along the road wealthy mainlanders have purchased lots and built homes, creating *haole* islands amidst the east Maui landscape. The community is growing but hardly changing. New residents have imported their own standards and life-styles, but they have often joined with cowboys, road workers, and hotel waitresses to block envi-ronmentally unsound developments in and around Hana.

Take the left-hand turn to Hamoa, past Koki Beach (named after my son), around the corner and along the shore to Hamoa Beach, the once-exclusive, salt-and-pepper sand beach where the hotel holds its luau. Try the beach yourself.

Continuing on, the road winds gracefully past isolated local Hawaiian homes, ranch parcels, and an occasional cow. Looking offshore on the left on a clear day, you can see Hawaii Island. In the early days, Hana was the site of many battles between the chiefs of the Big Island and Maui. Hamoa is where Kamehameha fought his first battle.

At the age of twenty-five, Kamehameha returned to Maui, the island where he was conceived, as a warrior in an invading army. On the gently sloping sweet-potato patches of Hamoa he fought with unusual bravery against the forces of Chief Kahekili—his father. He saved the life of his instructor in warfare when his tutor's feet became entangled in potato vines. While the tutor freed himself, Kamehameha held off attacking Maui warriors.

Beyond Hamoa, Oheo Gulch is where the Kipahulu Valley section of Haleakala National Park begins. Oheo has long been known as the Seven Sacred Pools. Twenty years ago I asked the social director at Hotel Hana-Maui where the name came from, and she told me she'd made it up to pique the curiosity of hotel guests. I've been trying to restore the correct name ever since, with little luck.

Sometime before the national park became a reality, I was taking an early-morning walk and scouting for picture possibilities along Oheo Stream, near where the mountain water from Kipahulu Valley slips into the last of many pools before it drops into the ocean. I noticed that several flagged stakes had been driven into the flat grassy area above the stream bank. They were survey stakes I hadn't seen before, delineating several connected rectangular spaces that looked suspiciously like a house site. It didn't take me long to decide what to do. I pulled all the stakes and threw them into the ocean.

I wondered which of the mainland visitors was planning to build a house on Oheo. Who would directly threaten the scenic integrity of Kipahulu Valley, and the public's access to

Wailua Falls

it, by building a house at Seven Pools? No matter how beautifully designed it might be, the house would be a desecration. I was outraged. Quickly I wrote an article for publication, telling the friends of Seven Pools that they should visit again soon, for their children might never be able to swim and play in Oheo Stream again, once the owner returned and replaced the stakes.

A retired Pan Am executive phoned me shortly afterward. It was his house. He said he had no intention of banning children from swimming in Oheo. I asked him to please build elsewhere and sell the land back to whomever he had bought it from. Within the month he had exchanged his parcel for a new house site on the other side of Kipahulu Valley.

I have always been a little miffed that I did not see the other waterfall before he found it. He told me of crawling on his hands and knees beneath a hau thicket and discovering the site. At dinner, which was served in the gazebo cantilevered over his stream, with spotlights directed on his own private waterfall, I enjoyed a carefully broiled steak while gazing covetously at the property. It would have made a nice addition to the future national park.

We became good friends, and he would often lend me his Land Rover so that I could drive into hard-to-reach places along the road and up the pasture. Once in the lower Kipahulu pasture meadow I met another car. We both stopped to exchange greetings. The other driver was Charles Lindbergh, my childhood idol. His wife, Anne Morrow, was with him. We quickly discovered a common bond in our environmental activism and agreed that all of Kipahulu Valley must eventually become a national park to prevent commercial exploitation and private ownership.

Lindbergh later wrote me about the magnificence of Maui, expressing well the concerns of an international conservationist: "What balance between good and evil our civilized ways will bring, we cannot now foretell; but experience shows that they destroy unprotected wilderness and wildlife with appalling ruthlessness; and that, unlike man's civilizations, destroyed nature cannot be rebuilt. Once violated it is gone forever, as is the ancient beauty of Waikiki Beach."

Lindbergh spent his last days in Hana. His grave lies on a promontory beside Palapala Hoomau Church, overlooking the ocean. An unfinished slab covers his grave by the chapel. To visit the grave site, continue about a mile past Oheo, watching for a whitewashed church through the trees. Turn left when you see it and open the gate. Drive down the dirt road for several hundred yards, keeping the fence on your left and turning left. Lindbergh's grave is under the trees in the churchyard.

In the Area

All numbers are within area code 808.

Hotel Hana-Maui: 248-8211

Hasegawa's General Store: 248-8231

10 ~

Maui's

Interior:

Paia-Makawao-
Kula Lodge-
Keokea-
Ulupalakua

How to get there: From Paia, take State 37 at Makawao. A few miles southwest of Makawao, turn left on State 377. From State 377, take State 378 to the summit of Haleakala. Returning to State 377 and State 37, continue south to Kokeo and Ulupalakua.

Highlights: *The Hui Noeau Visual Arts Center, Hawaiian cowboys in Makawao, Upcountry Protea Farm, Kula Lodge, Haleakala views overlooking all of central Maui, octagonal Holy Ghost Church, Ulupalakua Ranch country, Tedeschi Vineyards' Maui Blanc.*

The most appropriate place to begin this drive is Paia. Should you be starting out in the middle of the afternoon, as you head uphill toward Makawao you will meet swarms of cyclists coasting downhill. They are on the final leg of a day trip that began at dawn on the summit of Haleakala, 10,000 feet up.

On your left, just outside of town, is the only building of any historical significance on our trip. The light-blue masonry structure with the number 141 on the door is an old bank building, built in 1913, site of the first armed bank robbery in Hawaii. The road you're on, above the sugar mill, curves past many old estates and mansions. This was a choice neighborhood to live in during the years when sugar planters and pineapple magnates ran the island government and tourists didn't venture far from Honolulu's hotels. There were no hotels to speak of on Maui then. When visitors came over, they stayed as someone's guests. One of the few travelers to find his way this far out on the island was Mark Twain.

Before you reach Makawao, you will come upon the Hui Noeau Visual Arts Center, which may at first seem a little out of place. Located on one of these beautiful estates, called Kaluanui, the center was designed in 1917 by a Honolulu architect as a residence for the Maui Baldwin family, who lived there until the mid-1950s. Near the entrance to the nine-acre estate are the remains of an early mule-powered sugar mill, one of the first to use a centrifugal to separate sugar crystals.

Makawao presents a decidedly Western aspect, with its battered buildings and false-front stores. The town serves as the central meeting point for the high country's cowboys, or *paniolos*, as you can easily verify by dropping in at the corner bar on any Saturday night. The *paniolos* put on a wild and wonderful rodeo for several days every Fourth of July weekend in the local corral, preceded by a morning parade up Main Street.

Try the Casanova Italian Restaurant, one of the area's few night spots, if you're coming through in the evening. In the early morning, stop for a treat at the popular Komoda Store bakery.

Drive on straight up the hill, through the main intersection, past Pookea Church on the right and the entrance to Maunalei private girls' school. Turn right at the highway junction onto Hanamu Road and proceed west into the eucalyptus forest. These tall, straight trees are eucalyptus robusta, the timber trees that California thought it was getting from Australia but Hawaii got instead. They are a hardwood, termite proof, often used in Hawaii for flooring, cabinetwork, and custom furniture. Entire houses have been built of the wood.

Turn left when you reach the main Kula Road going uphill. You are on Haleakala Ranch. Go past the jacaranda trees, and watch carefully for the turnoff to Upcountry Protea Farm at the point where the first buildings appear. The paved drive, Kimo, travels straight up the hill for a mile to the farm entrance. You'll find hundreds of fantastic protea flowers to wander around in. Great place for pictures of a seemingly unlimited variety of blooms.

Protea is a flower of South African origin that thrives in Kula country, where the climate is similar to that of its native land. It is very much at home in the volcanic soils of Haleakala. Protea has become such a part of Maui's life-style that virtually everyone thinks of it as a typical Hawaiian plant. You'll see displays of its large flowers—in all styles, shapes, and colors—on every hotel banquet table. You may even find a single protea blossom on your cafe table.

Around a couple of turns farther on, *makai* (seaward) of the main Kula Road, is Kula Lodge, which has seen several owners and undergone many architectural changes over the years that I have been stopping by on my way to and from Haleakala. Today it may be better than ever, and I strongly urge you to stop for lunch or dinner. Relax by the fireplace with a planter's punch and enjoy this special place. Look out across all of central Maui, to the ocean on each side, west to Lanai Island, and northwest to Molokai. All sunsets here are incomparable, no matter what the weather.

An overnight stay would be even better. Kula Lodge has built rustic chalets complete with fireplaces, sleeping lofts, and sweeping views as good as those of the dining room. Each one is different. Here is a high-altitude retreat (elevation:

3,200 feet) that's worth the price. Downstairs below the main building is a gallery where a great Maui artist exhibits his works.

Drive on through the great high country of Kula, where the early plantation people came to get away from the heat of central Maui. Mountain ranchers lived here also, and in later years their cowboys built homes on smaller plots. Side roads are the entrances to mountain homes and farms; you'll see occasional flower and truck farms on the hillside.

Kula Botanical Gardens is an excellent place to stop for a picnic. Poisonous plants are highlighted in a side garden.

At Haleakala Junction is the turnoff to the summit, a twenty-two-mile side trip to the rim of Haleakala, which is a day's excursion in itself. There is another protea farm a short distance up the road. Watch out for the cyclists coasting down from the summit.

The side road, Waipolipoli, off the upper Kula Road, is only for the very adventurous with four-wheel drive and plenty of spunk. This ten-mile-long road, only the first half of which is paved, reaches a 6,000-foot-high ridge of Haleakala where a campground and cabin are located. Trails meander through a mature redwood forest that would make anyone from the Pacific West feel right at home. The redwoods were planted years ago when Hawaii was still a territory. Some forester back in Honolulu thought redwoods would grow well here. They do. The forestry people tested many trees—Monterey pine, Japanese sugi, Monterey cypress, and more eucalyptus—all of which now grow in profusion. From up here, high on Haleakala's west ridge, the view takes in Lanai, Kahoolawe, Molokai, and west Maui. It takes a while to look around here at the top of things, but there's no rush. Considering the quality of the road, you'll probably be the only people up here. There are miles of trails, including one lead-

Heliconia

ing all the way to the summit, although the main Haleakala entrance road will take you there much more easily.

Continuing along the upper Kula Road, Keokea is your last chance to gas up before going on to Ulupalakua Ranch. Since you will be returning this way, now is the time to locate the octagonal Holy Ghost Church on lower Kula Road. Turn right at the next junction and proceed until you see the freshly painted white church on the left. The church was hauled in by cart in pieces and reassembled here after a sailing ship brought the altar around the Horn in 1889. It was established to serve the Portuguese plantation workers living in Kula. Wood timbers support the tin cupola; the large gilded altar was carved in Austria. The church is still an important gathering place for the community.

Farther down the lower Kula Road and up Copp Road, just south of Kula Elementary School, the University of Hawaii Tropical Agricultural Experiment Station offers displays Hawaiian varieties of bedding plants, lots of roses, and a rare collection of ornamental protea. The flowers hold their color for weeks and retain their shape even after fading. Maui growers mail them to all parts of the world.

On to Ulupalakua Ranch country, 30,000 acres of rolling hills that begin as soon as Kula disappears. Herds of Angus and Hereford cattle and flocks of sheep graze up to the far ridge of Haleakala and down below to where open fields become subdivisions. The huge ranch uses a helicopter to help round up cattle in the spring. The company celebrates the roundup with a rodeo in one of the ranch corrals.

The road gradually angles southwest, past the ranch's headquarters and the ruins of Makee Sugar Mill. Here where sugar was produced in 1878, Tedeschi Vineyards is now making wine. Tedeschi began growing grapes in 1973 in partnership with the ranch and subsequently produced the first Hawaiian champagne, a commercial product with a faint blush of pink.

While his grapes were maturing, Tedeschi produced a very popular pineapple wine he called Maui Blanc. He said he would stop bottling this (in his opinion) inferior product as soon as his grapes began to ripen in quantity, but Maui Blanc sells so well that Tedeschi still keeps it in stock. He turned the old jail into a wine-tasting room, where you can sample Maui champagne. The jail's thick lava walls keep the temperature cool enough for wine storage; a trap door leads down to the dungeon, should cooler storage be needed.

In the Area

All numbers are within area code 808.

Hui Noeau Visual Arts Center: 572-6560

Komoda Store Bakery: 572-7261

Casanova Italian Restaurant: 572-0222

Kula Lodge: 878-1535

University of Hawaii Tropical Agricultural Station: 878-1213

Tedeschi Vineyards: 878-6058

11 ~

Maui's La Perouse Road:

Wailea-Makena-La Perouse Bay

How to get there: From Kihei, take State 12 to Wailea and Makena.

Highlights: *Big Makena and Little Makena beaches; La Perouse Bay, created by the most recent lava flow from Haleakala eruptions.*

This portion of Maui's west shore is the driest part of the island, receiving less than ten inches a year, which generally fall all at once. In past years it was considered a desert—kiawe-covered grasslands with an abundance of sunshine and afternoon winds to keep things reasonably cool. Developers saw great potential in this area, and after a water system was built, an entirely new resort was created in Wailea, a dry, sandy, supposedly uninhabitable part of Maui. Compared with the way the area looked fifty years ago, when the Marines practiced beach tactics here, the change can only be described as miraculous.

Drive out beyond the main Wailea hotels, keeping in mind that the Maui Prince Resort serves the most lavish buffet lunch of any hotel in Hawaii. Look for the side road down to Makena Church. It was not signed on my last visit and is therefore easy to miss, but the church is evidence that the missionaries at least found merit in the shore beyond Wailea.

In the days when Ulupalakua Ranch grew sugarcane, Makena was Maui's second biggest port. The freighters anchoring offshore were served by smaller craft carrying out sacks of sugar. It was a quiet, oceanside settlement of considerable quality. Even the owners of the ranch above maintained a residence on a rocky bluff overlooking the ocean at Makena.

Today, the country beyond the town is much like Makena was before development. The road, single-lane and mostly paved, curves like a trail, making it impossible to see oncoming cars at the top of hills and around curves. Blowing dust at times reduces visibility to a few yards. This is an excellent road for those who have not yet had the opportunity to drive across untouched lava fields. No one drives very fast here.

I would warn against driving on it when it is wet, but it rains so seldom that it is hardly worth mentioning. As the road proceeds it gets rougher and rougher; past the bay, it becomes very difficult for any one without a four-wheel drive. In fact, you have already gone too far if your rental car contract says anything about not driving on dirt, cinder, or coral.

As you pass Puu Olai, a cape about four miles beyond Wailea that you won't see very well through the kiawe forest, numerous dusty, rutted, side roads take off through the trees toward the ocean. Try anyone; they all lead to awkward parking places under the trees behind the beach.

The kiawe, which grows abundantly almost anywhere dry on the islands, is called mesquite in Texas, where it seldom

75

grows bigger than a large bush. In Hawaii it grows bigger than a house, with a trunk sometimes four feet in diameter. The tree has crooked, knock-kneed branches that drop nasty thorns and thrives where nothing else will grow. It's useless as a climbing tree—the branches bend down where they should go up. Many people consider the tree to be no more than an overgrown weed. Myself, I rather like it.

Kiawe is not the kind of tree you want to stroll under; fallen branches with inch-long thorns capable of piercing leather demand too much attention. Nor are kiawe much to look at. They are only good for looking through, but in this capacity they have no peer. Take the coconut. A grove of coconut is a forest of telephone poles. Or take the pink rainbow shower tree. When it's not covered with blossoms, the branches don't know what to do. It's a most awkward-looking tree. But the maze of barbed kiawe branches creates abstract masterpieces of whatever is viewed through them. Sunsets seen through the kiawe are particularly dramatic.

The beach beyond the kiawe is Big Makena, on Ahihi Bay. Directly offshore you'll see tiny Molokini Island, whose exceptional snorkeling waters can be visited in half-day tours from Wailea resorts. Beyond is Kahoolawe Island, up until a few years ago a noisy military bombing target, but today a quiet island watched over by Hawaiian activists who want their land back and the monarchy restored, a continuing controversy on all the islands.

Big Makena is a beautiful beach, excellent for sunbathing and picnicking. The swimming is best left to the skilled. It's better in the morning before the wind comes up. If you are so inclined, walk to the right along the shore, around the point to Little Makena, the clothing-optional beach.

Ahihi-Kinau, a state natural area reserve, encompasses the south end of the bay and Cape Kinau, an ecologically important area on both sides of the road. Although this arid landscape gives the impression of wasteland, it does possess unique natural resources. Unusual species of marine life thrive in the reserve's tidal pools and nearby waters: For example, twenty-three species of stony coral have been found. The ruins of Moanakala, a small fishing village on the bay, are being excavated by anthropologists.

The bay was named for the French explorer who anchored here briefly in 1786 before sailing on and disappearing at sea. At La Perouse Bay, the rough lava makes it difficult to get around, but the bay waters provide excellent snorkeling amid unusual marine life and submerged *pahoehoe* erupted from Maui's last volcanic activity in about 1790. The cinder cones you see on the hillsides of Haleakala, east of the shore, are the sources of the lava. From the air you can see a vast spread of lava not far beneath the water surface.

The track, as the road may more accurately be called beyond the bay, becomes rougher and more rocky as it continues along the shore through the lava fields. Park your car and continue on foot. The road, now little more than a trail, yields glimpses of ancient Hawaiian village life: stone walls protecting house platforms, walled canoe shelters, obvious remains of places where people lived, worked, and died. Few people have ever seen this place.

The Hawaiians' apparently sensitive and fragile relationship with their environment was suddenly disrupted by the arrival of foreign whalers and traders. The Hawaiians' feudalistic system, with its cruel punishments for such slight infractions of royal *kapu* as walking in the shadow of the *alii*, may conflict with the romantic impression many people have of these islands, but in retrospect the ancient days could well be described as idyllic.

The brutal *kapu* system was abolished by the Hawaiians themselves before the arrival of Boston missionaries, but in the wake of the missionaries came whalers and traders, who brought syphilis, measles, flu, rats, scorpions, cockroaches, and centipedes, with catastrophic consequences. Mosquito larvae were released deliberately when, after months at sea, frustrated crewmen dumped their water casks onto the Maui shore, protesting because native girls were prevented from swimming out to their ship.

For Hawaiians the foreign meeting was fatal. The dingy sails of alien ships signaled the advent of a new age, a new civilization that would turn their traditional way of life into a miserable existence. Yet once the first offerings of this civilization were imposed upon them, there was no turning back. The native Hawaiians stepped over the threshold of the new world with no defenses against the dangers that lay ahead.

Looking around, here where there are no trees and no obstructions of any kind for miles, we seem to be in a place where nothing has happened, but the orderly stonework and house sites tell otherwise. We are where much began in Hawaii—and much was lost.

In the Area

All numbers are within area code 808.

Maui Prince Resort: 874-1111

12 ~

Lanai:

Lanaihale-
Koele-
Munro Trail

How to get there: From Lanai City, take the road to Manele Bay, and turn left at a junction before the road descends to the beach. Ask at your hotel for precise directions to this junction.

Highlights: *Norfolk Island and Cook Island pines in Lanai City, the Lodge at Koele, George Munro's "drip forest" at the summit of Lanaihale.*

It is said of all the islands that each one is completely different from the others, but of Lanai it seems to be said more often. This is due in part to the fact that the island has been owned by one corporation, which has been growing only one crop since the early 1900s when Jim Dole planted his first pineapple. No other island has a Lanai City, 1,600 feet above sea level, with a climate like that of a California mountain town. On this island there are more pines than palms.

Lanai City is shaded by a stately collection of Norfolk Island and Cook Island pines planted by the pineapple company. There are no coconut palms here. There is absolutely nothing going on at night in Lanai City. Everything is quiet until the work whistle blows in the morning, as in any company town.

Everybody who lives on Lanai lives in Lanai City, and just about everyone who lives on Lanai works for the new hotels or Dole Pineapple, which is now in the process of phasing out the planting, growing, and harvesting of pineapple that began with their purchase of the island over seventy years ago. Before Dole, the island was a sheep and cattle ranch, and it appears to be returning to ranching, with additional jobs provided by two magnificent resort hotels— Manele Bay and the Lodge at Koele.

The best hotel on the island is the Lodge at Koele, built by Dole at the *mauka* (inland) edge of Lanai City next to the oldest and largest Cook Island pine on the island, planted in 1875. A *kamaaina* (native born) Hawaiian seeing the lodge for the first time would experience a sense of homecoming. The place looks as though it had been transported into the present from some earlier era in Hawaiian history. The inscription on the ceiling at the entrance reads, "In the center of the Pacific is Hawaii. In the center of Hawaii is Lanai. In the heart of Lanai is Koele."

The dining room overlooks a pool surrounded by white wicker furniture and rolling lawns that evoke the English countryside but with a soft Hawaiian accent. A Japanese gazebo and a Victorian-style glass conservatory overflowing with orchids draw your eye in the distance. The golf course, appropriately called "The Experience at Koele," lies beyond these structures. Everything is absolutely magnificent. Meals, menu, and room service should rapidly earn the Lodge at Koele a reputation that will keep it filled to capacity. Guests who stay in the luxurious rooms on the second floor will appreciate the services of their butler. This is the perfect spot for a stopover before going on to Lanaihale.

Although two new championship golf courses, seven

artificial lakes, and four tennis courts have been added to the island's recreational facilities, old-timers might be glad to know that the original nine-hole course is still open and still does not charge an entrance fee.

Lanai is not very large. You can get almost anywhere on the island in a day if all you want is a quick glimpse of the place. I am proposing only one excursion, an adventurous four-wheel-drive climb to the top of Lanaihale, 3,370 feet above sea level, from which you will be able to see almost every other island in Hawaii. You will enter an ecologically unique environment—everything you see growing along the way and on the mountaintop was planted for Dole by George C. Munro, a company naturalist who created the rainforest of Lanai.

Since it is always wet and muddy on top of Lanaihale, you need not be concerned if the weather is inclement when you set out. The trip will probably provide you with a good demonstration of how Hawaii's weather changes from morning to afternoon and different altitudes. Bring along a lunch for your stop at the summit. Remember that while the coast gets only four or five inches of rain a year and the Lodge at Koele gets about twenty, the annual rainfall at the summit of Lanaihale may be sixty inches or more. Wear your most casual clothes. You will get dirty and wet.

Native trees like ohia and koa can be seen along the way, but near the summit the road cuts through a dense forest of tree ferns, exotic tropical plants, and Norfolk Island pines—an evergreen forest. This may seem a strange botanical mixture to plant on a mountaintop, but Munro had a vision of creating a "drip forest" that would condense and hold water from the clouds hanging over Lanaihale every day. His ingenious idea worked. The water that was added to the island's groundwater reserves made possible everything that occurs on the island today—the pineapple, the people, and the resorts.

Kukui blossum

I'm convinced that the best route to travel is northward up the Munro Trail, so we will begin by taking the road to Manele Bay, turning off to the left at a junction just before the road descends to the beach. Lanai's roads are changing rapidly these days, so ask at the hotel for precise directions to this junction. The seven-mile road following the Munro Trail extends from the southeast near the area called Waiakeakua, up and across the mountain, and down to Koele's rolling grasslands.

The road, which is almost level at first, gradually becomes steeper until, near the summit, some of your passengers may prefer to get out and walk as you negotiate the final ascent. On the way, stop and look whenever you come to a break in the trees. See how many islands you can find in the panorama that unfolds from the mountain. Keep your eyes open for an overlook from which all of Lanai's pineapple fields can be seen. A picnic bench sometimes marks the spot.

As you travel down the north side, look for a trail leading off to a lookout 2,000 feet over Hauola Gulch, Lanai's deepest valley. Farther down, you will be able to look into Maunalei Gulch, where a pumping station takes water from the watershed that Munro improved and pumps it up and over the ridge into Lanai City. From the road you can also see notches in Hookio Ridge, which were carved out as defense bases for warriors during Kamehameha's 1778 invasion of Lanai, which ended in a massacre of Lanai natives. Various ridges and trails allow you to leave the beaten path briefly and experience nature at its unspoiled best.

The road winds down through a beautiful forest that slowly changes from tropical to temperate-zone vegetation as the altitude decreases. Wild turkey, pheasant, chukar partridge, and tiny axis deer, introduced to Lanai by Kamehameha's consul in Hong Kong before the turn of this century, now far outnumber the human population.

Some say the hunting on Lanai is better than on any other island in Hawaii. The State Department of Fish and Game regulates the sport and maintains the animal population at optimum levels for hunters and pineapple growers. Axis deer are fond of pineapples and will overrun the fields if their numbers aren't kept in check. When pheasant are shot in the pineapple fields, shotgun pellets can end up in the fruit.

On the lower slopes at Kanepuu you are in the last remaining portion of Hawaii's dryland forest, containing forty-eight species, including the endangered native Lanai sandalwood, Hawaiian gardenia, olopua (native olive), lama (native persimmon), fragrant huehue vines, maile, morning glory, and delicate yellow-orange ilima plants.

When you reach the Lanai cemetery, you're at the end of the Munro Trail. Turn left at the paved highway to return to the Lodge at Koele and a well-deserved rest.

Mark Twain described Hawaii as "the loveliest fleet of islands that lies anchored in any ocean." Of Hawaii's rainbows he wrote: "These charming spectacles are present to you at every turn; they are as common in all the islands as fogs and wind in San Francisco." At Lanaihale, you have reached the source of all Hawaii's rainbows.

In the Area

All numbers are within area code 808.

Koele Lodge: 565-7300

13 ~

Hawaii's Puna Loop:

Olaa-Pahoa-Kaimu-Isaac Hale-Kapoho-Honolulu Landing

How to get there: From Hilo, take the interstate to Keaau. Exit at Keaau and continue south on State 130 to Pahoa and on to Kalapana. Turn left at the new lava flow onto the graded Puna shore road to drive to Opihikao and points along the coast.

Highlights: *Volcano country, Black Sand Beach, the Painted Church, the Puna shore road, MacKenzie State Park with picnic tables carved out of lava slabs, Isaac Hale Park, Kapoho.*

Exit the volcano highway at Keaau and drive south. A mile beyond town, on the right, you'll see a magnificent New England–style home shaded by huge banyan trees. Built about 1920, this old sugar plantation manager's residence is one of the oldest homes in Puna.

Past Anahola, you come to Pahoa, an old sugar plantation town, on the branch road to the right. The sugar company has disappeared, but ragged stalks of sugarcane can still be seen struggling to grow along Puna roads. Pahoa started out in the late 1800s as a lumber town manufacturing koa and ohia railroad ties for the new Sante Fe Railroad's California mainline. After the trees were all gone, the land was converted to sugarcane fields. When sugar production was abandoned after the war, stands of anthurium, papaya, and macadamia were established. At a distance outside of town in the old forest, residents hid groves of *pakalolo* (marijuana), which at one time threatened to become the most valuable crop of all.

Today's Pahoans grow anthuriums, vanda orchids, papaya, bananas, and macadamia nut, and pump for hot lava to generate electricity. Pahoa is another of those Hawaiian towns where the original Oriental population has been replaced with mainland *haoles*. Seldom do you see a sign identifying an anthurium grower, but if you see a parking lot outside their netted growing areas, it is probably alright to stop and visit. Some growers like visitors, some don't. Yo Pizza, where I took a window seat to watch the town go by, had fresh orchid plumes on each table and served an excellent pizza for dinner. The chef doubled as the waitress.

Turn right at Pahoa School where the sign says the road is closed and drive on to Kalapana. This part of your trip no longer includes Hawaii Volcanoes National Park, because the connecting road is now covered with lava. At its highest point, the road crosses the Kilauea volcanic rift zone. On a cool morning, you will notice steam rising from cracks in the lava fields on both sides of the highway. You are entering volcano country.

This is an area I am very familiar with. For many years I have photographed Kilauea's eruptions for various publications. In the early 1950s, I was able to photograph the beginnings of a volcanic eruption for *Life* magazine. A volcanologist friend and I watched in amazement as the road to Kapoho quietly heaved and cracked before our eyes. The earth split open, creating black pits large enough for a car to fall into. The cracks continued along a jagged line into the adjacent field. Occasionally we would feel tremors through the soles of our boots. Civil defense and police evacuating local residents told us to leave. But with the photo opportunities developing all around me, I had to stay.

My rental car was full of film and cameras. Hanging everything on my shoulders, I ventured into the cane fields, stepping over the narrow cracks in the moist soil, which guided me along the rift zone. Then, straight ahead of me, wisps of steam from the nearest crack rapidly turned into a column of thick fumes. Lava began spurting into the air and overflowing a lengthening fissure in the earth. Increasing heat from the lava slowly piling into a spatter cone around the vent forced me to retreat. I learned later from scientists that the temperature of the new lava was perhaps 2,000 degrees Fahrenheit.

There was little danger from the vent itself as long as I could see, but as the fumes increased I became concerned. A sudden wind shift brought dense sulfurous fumes directly toward me. With my next breath, I sucked in hot sulfur gas. I ran until I collapsed in the clear, gasping for air. I learned my lesson. From then on, whenever I photographed erupting volcanoes I carefully stayed upwind.

Puna is quiet now, at least while this is being written, but Kilauea volcano has shown in past years that it is capable of producing more lava on very short notice—or none at all. Keep this in mind as you drive across the rift and down into Kalapana, which has recently been completely covered by lava from Kilauea.

The famous Black Sand Beach is covered with lava twenty feet high that came flowing down the coast on the ocean side in 1992. Queen's Bath, the marvelous pool in a lava crack, is gone. The national park campground and historical museum near Kamoamoa are gone. The county park at Kalapana is

Puna loop forest

gone. The people who lived here and their homes are gone. Kalapana's painted church was saved by foresightful local residents, who had it moved out of the reach of invading lava flows rather than risk losing it. For those who knew it, Kalapana is now a lonely place. Pele, the volcano goddess, destroyed it.

Walk in over the *pahoehoe* (smooth) lava if you like. You can go all the way to the shore if you're ambitious. After the lava has cooled, everything looks the same. In the cracks where the lava has bulged, fern fronds appear within a few days. Life eventually returns, but it will be a long time before anyone builds a home here again.

At the old junction where it was once possible to park and watch the surf roll in, a newly graded road allows you to turn left onto the Puna shore road. In this area, Puna is returning to life amidst 200-year-old lava. Burial sites and tombstones can be seen where there is no soil to dig. Trees and flowers have reappeared; there are even paved streets crossing the highway. Kalapana will be like this someday in the distant future.

Lava flows from Kilauea have also entered the area in recent years, some reaching the sea in great pyrotechnical displays and clouds of steam. You'll be driving over their solidified traces. Another flow may intrude tomorrow and render obsolete everything that I have written today.

Onward through increasingly beautiful and lush rainforest. The shore is pure South Pacific, with white waves crashing against the black, rocky shore and coconut palms arching gracefully over the surf. Passing Opihikao you enter rural Hawaii, picture-postcard country, with the necessary white New England church (the Reverend John Makuakane, pastor), and very little else. No tour buses come this way. You are the only visitors to this paradise.

Look for a black sand beach below. Look under the coconut palms for baby palms starting from fallen nuts. Explore MacKenzie State Park, a wonderful place to stay the night, should you have overnight gear with you. Check out the picnic tables and benches made of *pahoehoe* lava slabs. A section of the King's Highway, a round-the-island trail built by Kamehameha, passes through the park, forested here with a grove of ironwood trees so dense that neither sun nor rain can penetrate.

At the next intersection, turn right to Isaac Hale Park, an old-time beach park slated for improvement since the destruction of Kalapana Beach. The bay is generally too rough for launching boats or swimming, but the surfers will be out if the waves are up. Walk around to the right, past the caretaker's house, to the head of the bay. Keep your eye out for a path into the jungle, where a very pleasurable discovery awaits you. You'll find a freshwater pond, about fifteen feet in diameter, heated by volcanic rocks. This natural pool is rimmed with pandanus trees whose branches nearly touch overhead, creating a tropical glade in the jungle. Take off your clothes and get in. There is one unwritten law: No soap!

Before the next junction, Puna's jungle has disappeared, and only lava can be seen. There is nothing but lava in all directions at the crossroads where a library and school building once stood. The town of Kapoho used to be up the road to the left about a mile—an entire plantation town immolated in one night.

Farther along, the shore road enters the tropical forest through a tunnel of giant mango trees, hanging vines, bird's-nest ferns, coconut palms, pandanus, and every other species that Puna has to offer. Drive slowly and savor the experience.

The road is unpaved, rough in places, but easily passable in a sedan. Where the road comes closest to the shore, you have arrived at Honolulu Landing. Stay a while before venturing back to the civilized world.

14 ~

Hawaii's Kohala Mountains:

Waimea-Hawi-Pololu-Kawaihae

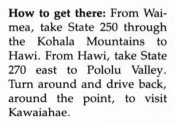

How to get there: From Waimea, take State 250 through the Kohala Mountains to Hawi. From Hawi, take State 270 east to Pololu Valley. Turn around and drive back, around the point, to visit Kawaiahae.

Highlights: *Views of Mauna Kea, Mauna Loa, and Hualalai from a beautiful mountain road; the land of Kamehameha the Great's birth; Pololu Valley Lookout.*

Your excursion begins in the town of Waimea, headquarters of Parker Ranch, the largest privately owned ranch anywhere. All the cattle you see, no matter where you look, belong to Parker Ranch. Waimea looks the way it does because the owner of Parker Ranch, Richard Smart, thought that was the way it should look. He even supplied the paint to help move things along. After he died, a local *hui* (partnership) took over the management of the spread, and changes are gradually occurring. But there are no beaches or high-rise hotels and winters here are cold and windy, so the place will probably stay much as it is—a cowboy town.

Take State 19 through town. For local flavor, the best place for breakfast is Masayo's, on the main street beyond the park. For lunch, the Hawaii Bread Depot will satisfy. For coffee, try Waimea Coffee Country, and for dinner take a table at one of the best eating places in America, Merriman's, the white building on the corner. (Be sure to make reservations.) How this great restaurant ended up in Waimea I don't know. The owner is the chef—you can watch him and his assistants at work in the kitchen.

Every Hawaiian island has more than one place called Waimea, but this Waimea had two names for a time: Waimea and Kamuela (meaning Samuel in Hawaiian), in honor of one of founder Parker's grandsons. For a while both names were used, until the post office and airport decided on Kamuela. Now the zip code is Kamuela and the town is Waimea.

At the junction of State 250 and State 19 is Kamuela Museum, a private collection of island artifacts. Proceed straight ahead on State 250 into the Kohala Mountains. On the right you'll pass the Hawaii Preparatory Academy, the most expensive private school in Hawaii.

Ahead of you, as the narrow road climbs upward, a picturesque drive leads through the lush ranchlands of Kohala to the plantation town of Hawi. Nothing that you see along the way—not one tree, bush, flower, cactus, or blade of grass—is native to this soil. Captain George Vancouver imported cattle, goats, and sheep to the island for King Kamehameha, who ordered that his cattle be allowed to roam free through the countryside. The new arrivals soon mowed down the native Hawaiian plants. The livestock scheme was a mistake, but it made possible Parker Ranch. The vegetation you see was brought in from elsewhere.

The cactus, originally a spineless variety propagated in California, was brought to the ranch as possible cattle feed. It

Waimea Parker Ranch in the Kohala Mountains

quickly changed its growing habits in Hawaii and the spines returned, making it useless for its intended purpose.

The grass grows thick in this moist climate. Shaded by ironwood trees, this little-used road passes through perpetually green rangelands dotted with smoothly contoured, grass-covered cinder cones.

Along the way, at Kahua Ranch, visit the tiny Protestant church with fresco murals by John Charlot, on a side road high on the hillside. Enjoy a picnic in the roadside grass anywhere you can find your way through the fence. No matter how hot it is in hotel country on the shore, the weather will be cool and pleasant in the Kohala Mountains, if somewhat cloudy in the afternoon. And the views are all panoramic.

Mauna Kea (altitude: 13,796 feet) is especially impressive in February, when it is covered with snow down to its lower slopes. Look carefully on a clear day and you will see the bumps of observatory buildings on the highest summit. The Mauna Loa summit and Kona's Hualalai are also in view. In the opposite direction, as the downhill road begins, you'll be able to make out Haleakala on Maui Island across Alenuihaha Channel.

As you head downhill into Hawi, you enter old plantation country, the home of Kohala Sugar in years past. Bob Krauss, writing in Hawaii's first guidebook, likened Kohala to "an old attic filled with dusty treasures that had a haunted-house fascination." Your first sight of Hawi will bear him out. The old wood buildings are still standing, but the community of Hawi did not survive the closing of the sugar mill in 1970. In this isolated area, sugar had been the only business for almost a century. Take a peek at the Takata Store and Naka-hara Store if you like old country stores.

This is the land where Kamehameha the Great, who brought the islands of Hawaii under one rule in 1795, was born. This northern edge of the island was the seat of the kingdom during his reign. Mookini *Heiau*, near the old airport, is one of the four largest *heiaus* in Hawaii. In more recent years, the first railroad system in the islands operated here, linking sugar mills with the harbor down the coast at Mahukona.

The original statue of King Kamehameha is located here, at Kapaau, along the road to Pololu Valley. The original was lost when the ship transporting it from Italy sank. A duplicate was ordered by the kingdom, but before it reached the islands, the original statue was found standing in front of a general store in the Falkland Islands, where it had been salvaged from the sunken ship. The original was purchased and carried back to Hawaii for installation in Kohala, since Honolulu already had the duplicate.

The hiking trail beginning at the Pololu Valley overlook belongs to a network of trails built as part of Kohala Sugar's extensive water system, which ran along the Kohala Coast. These spectacular trails are no longer open to the public, which is a great shame. They were cut out of the sides of vertical canyons and pass under waterfalls, over white-water streams, and through mountain meadows. Along the way, complete multibedroom homes were built for the ditch tenders. One house in Pololu Valley boasts a six-foot-long bathtub. I remember asking how the tub was brought in. Answer: They simply put a cork in the drain and floated the tub in to Pololu in the ditch.

It is possible to walk into Pololu Valley on the trail at the end of the road, but it is in very bad shape, barely suitable for mules. Experienced hikers can make the mile-long trip to the black sand beach. No one lives in Pololu Valley. Ancient taro patches were destroyed in the 1946 tsunami wave.

State 270 returns through Hawi and along the shore to Mahukona and Kawaihae Harbor. En route is the turnoff to

Upolu Airport and Kamehameha's birthplace, Kamehameha Akahi Aina Hanau, and Mookini Luakini *Heiau*. Both sites are hard to reach, down a two-mile-long dirt road, off the paved airport road, that turns into mud when it rains. It's best to come by on Kamehameha Day, June 11, when special celebrations and cultural programs are presented.

The facilities at Kapaa County Park are in disrepair, but the waters offshore offer some of the best snorkeling to be found anywhere, according to connoisseurs of the sport.

A little farther on, you'll find Lapakahi State Historical Park, which may seem disappointing at first glance. The Lapakahi area has been selected for an extensive archaeological study of the ahupuaa, the old Hawaiian system of land division. The prehistoric remains of sweet potato tubers have been discovered here. Evidence of village life has even been uncovered offshore, beneath the sea, where a fifteenth-century coastal village now lies submerged.

Leave Lapakahi early. The entry sign posts the warning: "This gate locked at 4:00. If locked in call police 889-6225. Nearest public phone 7½ miles north on 170." That's almost all the way back to Hawi—a long walk.

The discovery and settlement of Hawaii brought to an end the great ocean migrations begun in Asia nearly 3,000 years earlier. The Polynesians, as far as we know, undertook no further ambitious ocean expeditions after they reached Hawaii. Did they attempt to explore eastward? We don't know. Surely they found it cold when venturing north of Hawaii. Perhaps they concluded that Hawaii was indeed the land of the gods—their ultimate goal.

Hawaii Island was a fertile land, with ample water, plentiful fish, and abundant natural resources. The Polynesian explorers stayed on their islands and became Hawaiians, creating a new language and culture, new arts and religious rituals, and an unwritten literature passed down in *meles* (chants) and songs.

Just before reaching Kawaihae there is a gulch, Honokoa. Many years ago several friends and I wandered up this valley in search of a burial cave. We wanted to see for ourselves some of the Hawaiian carved images and other artifacts we had heard of or seen on display at the Volcano Park visitors' center. Maybe we would find the famous Forbes' Cave. We weren't sure.

We found a cave opening, high on the side of the gulch. Clearing away fallen branches and boulders, we crawled inside a narrow passage that curled downward, then outward and up, and finally opened into a large space. We looked about us. Pieces of the cave ceiling had fallen about on the objects gathered there. An outrigger canoe lay along the wall ahead. On all sides were skulls stuffed with tapa cloth. Carved wooden images reflected our lights. This must have been an important burial cave containing the remains of high-ranking *alii*. Although I had lugged in all my equipment, intent on photographing the cave and its contents, I could not bring myself to take even one picture. Suddenly I had to get out of there. I struggled back through the cramped passage to the outside where I could breathe again. I never ventured inside another burial cave again.

In the Area

All numbers are within area code 808.

Masayo's: 885-4295

Kamuela Bread Depot: 885-6354

Waimea Coffee & Country: 885-4472

Merriman's: 885-6822
Kamuela Museum: 885-4724
Takata Store: 889-5261
Nakahara Store: 889-6359

15 ~

Hawaii's Chain of Craters Road:

Halemaumau- Kilauea Iki- Kamoamoa

How to get there: Take State 130 to Hawaii Volcanoes National Park.

Highlights: *Halemaumau fire pit, sunrise touching Mauna Loa, Thurston Lava Tube, a forest of ferns, craters and spatter cones, miles of lava fields.*

In the Volcanoes Park area, there are two great places to spend the night. Gordon and Joann Morse run My Island Bed and Breakfast. Start your day with their all-you-can-eat breakfast. Almost next door is Kilauea Lodge, which offers atmosphere and top-flight meals.

Get out on the edge of the caldera at dawn. (A caldera is a large, steep-sided depression formed when a volcano collapses on an emptied magma chamber.) On cold mornings steam issuing from vent cracks on the right will be flowing down the caldera wall like a ghostly waterfall. The caldera floor is covered with steam rising from cracks in the surface. As the sun rises, the steam disappears, and the caldera is transformed into a black abyss, quiet and deadly, with Halemaumau at the center of it all. Above, the first sun strikes the summit of Mauna Loa, wrapping the mountain in a reddish glow, which slowly softens to pastel shades of gold as the day begins. Also watch the full moon set behind Mauna Loa.

Volcanoes Park is morning country, where giant tree ferns are partially hidden in the swirling fog still hanging around from Hawaii's volcanic birth. From the hotel, drive toward Mauna Loa, passing turnoffs to the sulfur beds on the right and steaming cracks on the left. Continue, bearing left until you reach the Volcano Observatory, directly overlooking Halemaumau. Here you'll learn about volcanoes and eruptions, and you'll be able to see the seismographic wake of last night's earthquake.

You drive over great cracks and rifts in the caldera surface, some cracks quite old, some new. On the floor of Kilauea you can park in a paved parking lot and watch the lava flows from your car. Sort of a drive-in volcano. From here walk to the edge of Kilauea's fire pit, Halemaumau. Sometimes a boiling lava lake, steaming and threatening, but most often quiet, Halemaumau did not exist before 1924, when a gigantic steam explosion blew out the hole, throwing giant basaltic boulders over the caldera floor and killing a local photographer, the only volcano fatality known.

Climbing upward on the access road, you pass through more recent lava flows and spatter cones into an ohia lehua forest. Don't turn onto the Chain of Craters road yet. You'll return to this junction. First you must see the fern forest.

The native hapuu ferns are fifteen feet high along the trail to Thurston Lava Tube, a volcanic tunnel formed when the surface of a lava flow cooled and its molten interior drained away. In the cool mist, complex, delicate ferns contrast with the tall, straight ohia lehua trees. Close up, the ferns display an infinite variety of interlocking fronds mixing in geometric patterns. New fern buds uncurl covered in a fuzzy red froth that was used to stuff pillows in ancient times.

A short distance back down the way you came is Kilauea Iki and the Devastation Trail, a walk along the edge of the ohia forest destroyed by the eruption of Kilauea Iki. For several days it rained hot lava, the cinder strewn all about. Where they managed to stay upright, the trees are slowly recovering.

Look into the undamaged forest for ohelo berries, red, pink, or yellowish fruit growing on a low bush. The ohelo berry resembles a blueberry in size and form and tastes rather like a cranberry. Ohelo can be eaten raw but are much better baked in a pie with sugar and lemon juice. The plant is sacred to Pele.

Return to the Chain of Craters junction and continue along the Kilauea rift, a grand collection of old fire pits, lava flows, craters, and other remnants of Kilauea's fiery activity. Nowhere else in the world can you drive so near a volcano at work and see the edge of the earth being created out of molten rock. There are craters on both sides of the road where magma chambers collapsed long ago. In recent years Kilauea has erupted again in its old craters, pouring lava over the sides.

Old roads covered by lava have become parking areas for new trails into the new lava country. Within sight of Mauna Ulu, which erupted in 1973, walk to the end of the road and onto the short trail (two miles round trip) to the top of Puu Huluhulu overlooking the *pahoehoe* (smooth lava) fields surrounding the cinder cone. From the top of Huluhulu, you can see the 770-foot-high cone of Pu'u Oo, five miles away, which erupted forty times between 1983 and 1986, pushing lava fountains as high as 1,500 feet. The eruption could be seen from Hilo and created a new volcanic peak in the national park. By 1992, lava from this eruption and nearby vents was slowly flowing to Kalapana, where over 200 homes and build-

Fern forest road

ings were destroyed, and 300 acres of land were added to the island of Hawaii.

The Chain of Craters road has been rebuilt several times after lava flows from new Kilauea eruptions covered and destroyed miles of paved surface. Pele, the goddess of fire and volcanoes, has played with the road often, as might have been predicted when the new highway was first opened. Before these eruptions, the Chain of Craters road went all the way to Kalapana, connecting with the Puna Highway. The park museum along this route is now buried, its steel roof frame casting grotesque shadows on the lava. The first *heiau* (shrine) built on the island has escaped destruction—for now.

As the road turns toward the ocean, curving through a deep cut, a vast panorama of lava flows and ocean comes into view—a landscape of glistening waves, wind-tossed water, and miles of *pahoehoe* lava fields. In the distance, where Kalapana once was, more lava continues into the ocean haze.

You'll find many parking turnoffs along the way. Some offer trails to petroglyph fields; others are simply well-placed lookouts where you can stop and stare at the awe-inspiring landscape around you. The lava cliff drops vertically into rough waves dashing against the shore. In the distance you will see great clouds of steam rising from the ocean if Kilauea lava is pouring into the ocean.

When you arrive on the ocean road, the park service will tell you where to park. It is impossible to predict any eruption, but if one is in progress when you visit—and there have been many over the last several years that Kilauea has been pouring lava onto Kalapana and Kamoamoa—the park service will have made a cross-country trail over the old *pahoehoe* lava toward the new lava. Start walking late in the afternoon, just before twilight, the best time to view the greatest show on earth.

Volcanic activity not only is adding to the island of Hawaii, extending the shore outward foot by foot, it is also in the process of creating another island offshore. Nine miles out, scientists have located another volcanic island in eruption. Loihi, as this island is known, has about 3,000 feet to go before it breaks through to the surface, sometime in the next 20,000 years. The new island beneath the sea is already 11,200 feet high, and has produced a summit caldera the size of Kilauea's with two craters on top.

One quick glance does not reveal the hidden excitement of Volcanoes Park. The tremendous forces of nature generally lie dormant, only occasionally bursting through the crust. Quiet wisps of steam escape to remind us of how hot things are only a short distance beneath our feet. Look closely and you will see creation at work.

In the Area
All numbers are within area code 808.

My Island Bed & Breakfast: 967-7216
Kilauea Lodge: 967-7366
Volcano House: 967-7321

16 ~

Hawaii's Kona Belt Road:

Kaloko-Holualoa-Kealakekua-Honaunau

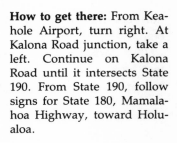

How to get there: From Keahole Airport, turn right. At Kalona Road junction, take a left. Continue on Kalona Road until it intersects State 190. From State 190, follow signs for State 180, Mamalahoa Highway, toward Holualoa.

Highlights: *Coffee tasting along the Kona belt road, 1,500 feet above sea level; arts and crafts in Holualoa; the Painted Church; the Captain Cook Monument; bougainvillea and sacred heiaus.*

Kona doesn't look like much from the Keahole Airport—just miles of lava leading up to Mount Hualalai, an ordinary-looking mountain. But between the airport and the mountain there is glorious country and lots of sunshine. This area has been lived in for a thousand years because everything grows so well here: coffee, macadamia nuts, fish, and bananas. *Mauka* it rains a lot—*makai* it seldom rains until sunset, so the coffee country gets morning sun followed by afternoon shade—a useful arrangement.

Kona is a little wild in appearance, a grand example of free enterprise at work, as if each property owner deliberately chose to do something completely different. No one seems to have heard of zoning; they just build it. This is a community unlike any other in Hawaii. Kona is not concentrated in any one area; rather it is spread out haphazardly in subdivisions, small ranches, large ranches, farms of every kind, just plain acreage, individual homes, and shops.

Turn right upon leaving the airport, and then take a left at Kalona Road junction. In typical Kona fashion, one of the best restaurants around can be found in the Kaloko Industrial Park to your right. Sam Choy, a former Hilton chef, has set himself up in a warehouse with glass walls and serves wonderful food.

With a grand, satisfied feeling, continue up Kalona Road to where it intersects with State 190 coming in from Waimea. If you would like to see the lower elevation of Hualalai, continue upward as far as you like, on a recently paved road rising into Hawaiian cloud forest, through forests of hau and ohia lehua, hapuu fern and island lobelia. The road goes even higher, but stops well short of the 8,000-foot-high summit of Hualalai.

Continuing on State 190, ignore signs for Kailua, and turn left onto Mamalahoa Highway, toward the town of Holualoa. The belt road begins here, winding southward through old Kona coffee country for twenty miles. The road is narrow and slow, so you won't miss anything along the way. Watch for wild turkeys crossing the road. Bright red poinsettias will still be blooming in March. No matter what the time of year, practically everything will be blossoming. The bougainvillea and hibiscus are always beautiful.

After a couple of miles, the first building you come to, on your right, will be the Onizuka store, the home of Ellison Onizuka, who grew up here, worked in the store as a boy, and died in the Challenger space shuttle explosion. The store is usually closed now, but until recently Onizuka's eighty-year-old mother still opened the store for local residents. If the store happens to be open, drop in.

You'll see coffee growing on both sides of the road. When the beans are red, they're ripe and ready to be picked by hand. Most coffee beans ripen during the winter months. During the years when coffee was king in Kona, schoolchildren had their big vacation in the winter so that they could help pick coffee. During coffee-harvesting season, bags of dry coffee beans will be stacked along the road, waiting for roasting-mill trucks.

The first possible stop for a cup of coffee along the way will be at the Hawaiian Mountain Gold Coffee Shop, run by the Ferrari family from Italy. That's their Rolls Royce parked in front. The Italian auto maker was their great-grandfather.

The next coffee shop, the Holualoa Cafe and Espresso Bar, in the funky old town of Holualoa, serves coffee and light lunch. Across the street is the Holualoa Kona Hotel, perhaps the oldest hotel in Kona, and still in business. On my last visit, single rooms were $15, doubles were $23, including room tax—the lowest hotel rate in Hawaii. Goro Inaba, owner and manager, says he doesn't serve meals anymore and may raise rates in the near future, but his prices will still be the lowest around. The rooms are simple, without television or telephone, but the roof doesn't leak and the nights are quiet.

Across the street and down the hill a bit are the Holualoa Art Galleries, in the old wood shop building. There are eight art galleries in town. The Kona Arts Center, with the gravel floor at the entry, showcases works by local artists and offers classes that may be in session the day you look in. The Coffee Mill Workshops are for art, not drinking coffee. This old coffee town is quietly emerging as Kona's leading arts and crafts center.

Look for Tom Gouvias's old "Butcher Shop," recently renovated by local Boy Scouts. It was an old post office before it became a butcher shop. Paul's place across from the post office sells groceries; the store bulletin board has something for everyone.

After the State 11 junction, continue straight ahead. On the right is Kimura's Lauhala Shop, which has been doing business here for decades, selling the best of woven lauhala baskets, purses, bags, and authentic local handicrafts—not imports. A little farther on, you'll come to Doris's Place.

As you drive along, you'll see traces of the old days of the coffee business: bits and pieces of drying racks, storefronts, and the remnants of individual farms. The road crosses large-capacity culverts and high bridges, for it does rain heavily at times on summer afternoons. Teshima's Fine Foods is here, a popular local restaurant, often filled with tourists driving up from their hotels along the coast. The traffic increases in both directions as you join the main highway south.

At Kainaliu, look for the pretty Shingon Buddhist Mission, Kona Koyasan Daishiui, up on the hillside above the rows of orange lantern posts and plumeria trees. Stop in at the Oshima Store and the Aloha Theater Cafe. No movie anymore, but a good, healthy, plain lunch. Kainaliu has many coffee shops. Try Jack Ass Kona Coffee—you can smell the beans roasting from quite a distance.

In the next town, Kealakekua, look for the Kona Historical Society, housed in the historic Greenwell Store, where you can browse through Kona Coffee photos of the 1800s and historic displays featuring early Kona history. The museum is part of the old Greenwell Ranch, a kamaaina family of the old days. Find the Little Grass Shack at Kealakekua, with the new corrugated steel roof. It's filled with a fine collection of Hawaiiana, arts and crafts, and gifts.

The old stone Kealakekua Church is where I was married some time ago. They offer Sunday services in three languages: English, Filipino (Ilocano), and Japanese. I was married in English.

The Kealakekua Art Center features several art galleries. If you're hungry, try the Peacock House Chinese Restaurant or the Gallery Cafe.

Watch for the right turn to Kealakekua Bay and turn downhill for four miles of really narrow, winding road with panoramic ocean views at every curve. Don't let the drivers behind you bother you; Napoopoo Road offers plenty of wide spots where you can pull over and admire the view. Take the side road on Middle Keei Road to St. Benedict's Church, located on the hill above. This is the famous Painted Church of Kona, a rickety wooden chapel embellished by a devoted priest.

The Mauna Loa Coffee Mill and Museum is on the way to Napoopoo. Stop here for a free sample of freshly brewed Kona coffee right out of the roaster, and watch how your coffee goes from berry to bean to bag. If you haven't sampled Kona coffee yet, do it now. At the bottom of the hill, turn right, to where the road ends at Kealakekua Bay. Napoopoo is the birthplace of Henry Opukahaia, who sailed to New England aboard one of the earliest trading ships to visit the islands, and who in Boston inspired the first American missionaries to sail to Hawaii in 1820.

The stone work you see rising above the parking area is the outer wall of the restored Hikiau *Heiau*, overlooking the bay. Before he was killed by the Hawaiians, Captain James Cook performed a Christian burial service here for one of his crewmen. Across the bay, on the opposite low shelf of land, is a white spire, the Captain Cook Monument, marking the spot where Captain Cook died in 1779 during a struggle with a native who had stolen one of his small boats. Cook was killed—and, some say, eaten—by Hawaiians who had earlier welcomed him as the god Lono.

The bay is one of those rare places in the world where spinner dolphins swim close to shore, and it is used by dolphins for resting, breeding, giving birth, and nursing their young. The bay offers an undisturbed environment critical to their survival.

Driving south through the narrow streets and stone walls of Napoopoo Village, you pass into open country belonging to the Bishop Estate. As you near Honaunau Bay, watch for a road bearing right. Take it down to the shore where locals keep their canoes and canoe trailers. Visitors and locals will be out on the black shelf of *pahoehoe* at Honaunau, sunbathing, fishing, and snorkeling. Scuba divers also use the shelf as a platform.

Drive up the paved road, staying to the right, and keep your eyes open for Bong Brothers' fruit stand and parking area for the important Pu'uhonua o Honaunau National Historic Park (formerly called the City of Refuge). This site contains the best-preserved *heiau* (shrine) in the islands; and park service historians provide information and self-guided tour maps. You'll find a restored *heiau*, wood tiki images, and canoe sheds. During Hawaiian cultural events the park presents authentic arts and crafts demonstrations by Hawaiians. It was in sacred places like Pu'uhonua that Hawaiian *kahunas* (priests) forgave those who had violated royal taboos. After the offender had succesfully crossed the bay, he would reach inside the Great Wall and take refuge at the *heiau*. Menacing wood idols at the shore made this one of Hawaii's most sacred spots. Built to traditional specifications, the ancient architecture at this site is ranked among the finest in the islands.

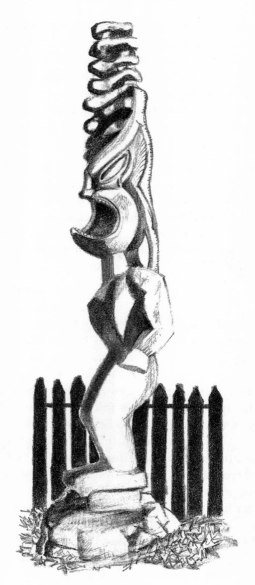

City of Refuge Historic Park

The highway to the belt road above is bordered by spectacular displays of bougainvillea, blooming profusely all year. Turn left when you reach the belt highway to return north along a road that provides grand vistas of the ocean below and flowering hillside above. Just before reaching Captain Cook town, look for the sign to the Amy B. H. Greenwell Ethnobotanical Garden, ten acres of upland countryside being developed by the Bishop Museum as a treasury for traditional Hawaiian plants. The garden is divided into six zones, with seaside plants and mountain trees, both wild and domestic species. Self-guided tours are free.

Try the Manago Hotel in Captain Cook if you want an inexpensive hotel room. Manago's dining room is a famous place. Everybody stops there for a coffeeshop meal of fried akule, a local fish. Then there is the Kona Plantation, which looks like a tourist trap, but makes good coffee.

When I first rode through Kona on the belt road in 1943, coffee sacks could be seen all along the road, waiting to be picked up. Coffee farmers were raking the beans on drying platforms in the sun. Donkeys stood waiting to carry coffee from the fields and dried coffee beans to roasting mills. That way of life has vanished, but Kona still has coffee, canoe races, marlin fishing, mom-and-pop general stores, and a laid-back style.

In the Area

All numbers are within area code 808.

Sam Choy's Restaurant: 326-1545
Holualoa Cafe and Espresso Bar: 322-9937
Kona Hotel: 324-1155

113

Holualoa Art Galleries: 322-8484

Kona Arts & Crafts Gallery: 329-5590

Kimura Lauhala Shop: 324-0053

Doris's Place: 324-4761

Teshima's Fine Foods: 322-9140

Oshima Store: 322-3844

Aloha Theater Cafe: 322-3383

Little Grass Shack: 323-2877

Kona Historical Society: 323-3222

Kealakekua Art Center: 323-3030

Peacock House Chinese Restaurant: 323-2366

Gallery Cafe: 323-3306

Mauna Loa Royal Coffee Mill and Museum: 328-2511

Amy Greenwall Ethnobotanical Garden: 323-3318

Manago Hotel: 323-2642

Kona Plantation: 328-8088

Glossary of Hawaiian Words

aa	rough lava
ae	yes
ahupuaa	land division extending from the uplands to the sea
aina	land
akamai	smart
ala	road
alii	royal, royalty
aloha	love, hello, farewell
aole	no
auwai	stream

auwe	alas!
hala	pandanus tree
hale	house
hana	work
hao	iron
haole	white person
hauoli	rejoice
heiau	temple
holoholo	to visit, run over
holoku	gown
honi	to kiss
hoomalimali	to flatter
huhu	angry
hui	club, partnership, society
hukilau	communal fishing
hula	dance
imu	ground oven
ipo	sweetheart
kahuna	priest
kai	sea
kalo	taro plant
kamaaina	native born
kanaka	male Hawaiian
kane	man
kapa	tapa cloth
kapu	forbidden, taboo
kaukau	food
keiki	child
kiawe	algaroba tree
Kokua	help
kona	south
koolau	north
kuleana	homestead plot
lanai	porch
lauhala	pandanus

laulau	bundle of food
lei	flower garland
lomilomi	massage
luau	feast
luna	plantation boss
mahalo	thank you
makai	seaward
malihini	newcomer
malo	loincloth
mana	spiritual power
manawahi	free
mauka	toward the mountains, inland
mauna	mountain
mele	chant
menehune	Hawaiian elf
moana	ocean
moe	sleep
muumuu	gown
nani	beautiful
niu	coconut
nui	big
oe	you
okolehao	ti root liguor
opu	stomach
pahoehoe	smooth lava
pake	Chinese
palapala	book
pali	cliff
paniolo	cowboy
pau	finished
pilau	smelly
pilikia	trouble
pipi	cattle
poi	taro paste
puaa	pig

puka	hole
pupu	hors d'oeuvre
pupule	crazy
wahine	woman
wikiwiki	hurry up

Index

119

Other titles in the Country Roads series:

Country Roads of Michigan
Country Roads of Massachusetts
Country Roads of Illinois
Country Roads of New Hampshire
Country Roads of Oregon
Country Roads of New York
Country Roads of Indiana
Country Roads of Ohio
Country Roads of Vermont
Country Roads of Washington
Country Roads of Quebec
Country Days in New York City
Country Roads of Kentucky
Country Roads of Pennsylvania

All books are $9.95 at bookstores.
Or order directly from the publisher (add $3.00
shipping & handling for direct orders):

Country Roads Press
P.O. Box 286
Castine, Maine 04421
Toll-free phone number: **800-729-9179**